Ferrell's

Ferrell's

MERYL DONEY

Jesus

THE MAN WHO CHANGED HISTORY

MERYL DONEY

Jesus

Designed by Graham Round

A LION BOOK

Oxford · Batavia · Sydney

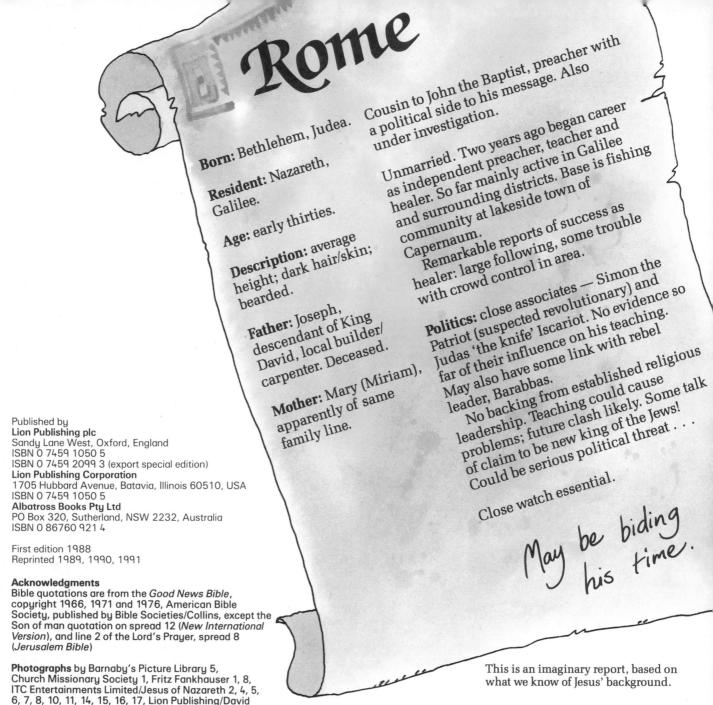

Rome

Born: Bethlehem, Judea.

Resident: Nazareth, Galilee.

Age: early thirties.

Description: average height; dark hair/skin; bearded.

Father: Joseph, descendant of King David, local builder/carpenter. Deceased.

Mother: Mary (Miriam), apparently of same family line.

Cousin to John the Baptist, preacher with a political side to his message. Also under investigation.

Unmarried. Two years ago began career as independent preacher, teacher and healer. So far mainly active in Galilee and surrounding districts. Base is fishing community at lakeside town of Capernaum.

Remarkable reports of success as healer: large following, some trouble with crowd control in area.

Politics: close associates — Simon the Patriot (suspected revolutionary) and Judas 'the knife' Iscariot. No evidence so far of their influence on his teaching. May also have some link with rebel leader, Barabbas.

No backing from established religious leadership. Teaching could cause problems; future clash likely. Some talk of claim to be new king of the Jews! Could be serious political threat . . .

Close watch essential.

May be biding his time.

This is an imaginary report, based on what we know of Jesus' background.

Published by
Lion Publishing plc
Sandy Lane West, Oxford, England
ISBN 0 7459 1050 5
ISBN 0 7459 2099 3 (export special edition)
Lion Publishing Corporation
1705 Hubbard Avenue, Batavia, Illinois 60510, USA
ISBN 0 7459 1050 5
Albatross Books Pty Ltd
PO Box 320, Sutherland, NSW 2232, Australia
ISBN 0 86760 921 4

First edition 1988
Reprinted 1989, 1990, 1991

Acknowledgments
Bible quotations are from the *Good News Bible*, copyright 1966, 1971 and 1976, American Bible Society, published by Bible Societies/Collins, except the Son of man quotation on spread 12 (*New International Version*), and line 2 of the Lord's Prayer, spread 8 (*Jerusalem Bible*)

Photographs by Barnaby's Picture Library 5, Church Missionary Society 1, Fritz Fankhauser 1, 8, ITC Entertainments Limited/Jesus of Nazareth 2, 4, 5, 6, 7, 8, 10, 11, 14, 15, 16, 17, Lion Publishing/David Townsend 1, 4, 5, 9, 10, 12, 14, Jean-Luc Ray 1, 8

Illustrations by Vic Mitchell 3 (temple), 4 (house), 6, 13 (soldier). All other illustrations by Graham Round and Kim Blundell

British Library Cataloguing in Publication Data
Doney, Meryl
   Jesus: the man who changed history.
   1. Jesus Christ — Juvenile literature
   I. Title
   232   BT202

ISBN 0–7459–1050–5

Library of Congress Cataloging-in-Publication Data
Doney, Meryl, 1942–
   Jesus: the man who changed history.
   1. Jesus Christ — Biography — Juvenile literature.
   2. Christian biography — Palestine — Juvenile literature.
   [1. Jesus Christ — Biography]   I. Round, Graham.
   II. Title.
   BT302.D59   1988   232.9'01 [B]   87–22857
   ISBN 0–7459–1050–5

Printed in Belgium

CONTENTS

Jesus lived in a small town in Palestine, nearly 2,000 years ago. He never went more than 300 km/200 miles from the place where he was born. He never owned a house, had a family, held an important position, or wrote a book. Some time around AD 33, he was arrested, tried and executed by the Romans as a trouble-maker.

Everything we know about his adult life could have been said and done in a matter of months. Yet many people would say he is the most influential human being who has ever lived.

Throughout the centuries since his death, countless men, women and children have been ready to live and die for him.

Today, one-third of the world's population call themselves followers of Jesus Christ, or Christians.

What makes this man so special?

Did Jesus really exist?

Most of the detailed information we have about Jesus comes from four books. They were written by Matthew, Mark, Luke and John and we call them the Gospels, which means 'good news'. Of these writers, Matthew and John were close friends of Jesus, who were with him right from the beginning of his work. Mark was a young man when Jesus died, but he knew the disciples and worked closely with their leader, Peter. Luke took great care to interview those who had known Jesus, before writing his history.

All four men wrote their books within about fifty years of Jesus' death, when people who knew him would still have been alive to check the facts.

Of course the actual pages they wrote have not survived, but in those days very careful copies of important books were made and passed from hand to hand.

The earliest copy found so far is a tiny piece of John's Gospel dated around ninety years after Jesus' death. Although this sounds like a long gap it is in fact much less than the gap between, for example, the life of Julius Caesar and the earliest historical documents about him.

The Gospels are part of the New Testament in the Christian Bible. They

were written by Jesus' followers, who wanted to tell the world about who he was and the marvellous things he did. When you read their books, they ring true because the accounts come from people who lived through the things they are telling about. The evidence is first-hand.

Today there are followers of Jesus — Christians — in countries all around the world.

These Indian children have drawn their own picture of Jesus.

What did Jesus look like?

We don't know anything for certain about how Jesus looked. None of the people who wrote about him mentioned it. They obviously didn't think it important.

Down the ages many artists have tried to picture Jesus. Most often, they imagine him as belonging to their own race and time. But it is almost certain that Jesus would have had the typical features and colouring of a man born in the Middle East.

Evidence from history

Apart from the Gospels, Jesus is mentioned by other writers of his day.

Josephus, a Jewish historian, writing in about AD 93:

'About this time there arose Jesus, a wise man, if indeed it be lawful to call him a man. For he was a doer of wonderful deeds, and a teacher of men who gladly receive the truth. He drew to himself many, both of the Jews and of the Gentiles. He was the Christ; and when Pilate, on the indictment of the principal men among us, had condemned him to the cross, those who loved him at the first did not cease to do so, for he appeared to them again alive on the third day, the divine prophets having foretold these and ten thousand wonderful things about him, and even to this day the race of Christians, who are named after him, has not died out.'

Tacitus, a Roman historian writing in about AD 115, looks back to the time when the Roman Emperor Nero made Jesus' followers take the blame for a terrible fire in Rome:

'Nero set up as the culprits and punished with the utmost refinement of cruelty, a class hated for their abominations, who are commonly called Christians. Chrestus, from whom their name is derived, was executed at the hands of the Procurator Pontius Pilate in the reign of Tiberius.'

In his 'Life of Claudius', **Suetonius** — private secretary to the Emperor Hadrian — talks of quarrels between the Jews and followers of 'Chrestus'.

The Jewish **Talmud,** written in the second century, speaks of Jesus' execution 'as a criminal'.

The earliest everyday mention of Jesus was discovered on two burial caskets dated between AD 40 and AD 50:

'Jesus woe!' (or 'Jesus, help!')

'Jesus, let him arise!'

These show that less than twenty years after his death, people were praying to Jesus, and looking forward to the new life after death which he promised.

★ Jesus was not born on 25 December in the year 0. Our calendar was worked out by a man called Dionysius the Younger about 500 years later, and he made a mistake in his calculations! Jesus was probably born around 7–4 BC.

★ Nazareth was not a sleepy little village. It was a busy town close to a main trade route.

★ The language Jesus spoke was Aramaic, an old Persian language. He could probably speak Hebrew and some Greek as well.

★ Jesus and his friends were used to a hard outdoor life. The distance from Lake Galilee, in the north, to Jerusalem was 160 km/100 miles and they would walk all the way.

BORN IN BETHLEHEM

For many people, the story of Christmas is a kind of fairy tale. It has everything — mother, father and the baby, three shepherds on one side, three kings on the other, stars, angels and even the arch-villain King Herod!

It is easy to forget that this was a real event involving real people.

Matthew and Luke, who wrote two of the Gospels, give details of what happened. Luke focuses on Mary; Matthew writes from Joseph's point of view.

Putting the two together, here is a summary of the main events.

★ Mary and Joseph, who lived in the town of Nazareth in the north of Palestine, were engaged to be married.

★ An angel messenger from God appeared to Mary, telling her that she would have a child — God's own Son.

★ An angel also appeared to Joseph, in a dream, telling him not to be afraid to marry Mary. He also told Joseph that the baby she was expecting should be called Jesus. (The name means 'rescuer', 'one who saves'.)

★ During her pregnancy, Mary visited her cousin Elizabeth, who was also expecting a baby. He would be Jesus' cousin, John the Baptist, sent to prepare people for Jesus' coming.

★ A census ordered by the Roman emperor forced the couple to travel to Bethlehem to register their names. There was no room for them to stay in the inn. When the baby was born, they wrapped him in strips of cloth and settled him to sleep in a manger where the animals were fed.

★ Shepherds on the hills outside the town were frightened when they saw an angel who told them about the birth of the baby. Suddenly the whole sky was filled with thousands of angels, all praising God. Immediately the shepherds set out to find the baby in the town.

★ Joseph and Mary named the baby Jesus. Later, they took him to the temple in Jerusalem to dedicate him to God.

★ While they were there, an old man named Simeon and an old woman called Anna both recognized the baby as someone very special. They said that here, at last, was the person God had promised to send to rescue his people.

★ Some men from the East, who studied the stars, came to Jerusalem. They were looking for a baby whom they believed would grow up to be the king of the Jews. King Herod sent them on to Bethlehem, where they found the baby and gave him gifts of gold, frankincense and myrrh. They were warned in a dream not to go back to the jealous king, who intended to kill the baby.

★ Also in a dream, Joseph was told to take his family into hiding in Egypt.

★ King Herod, determined to destroy the baby king, ordered the death of all baby boys in and around Bethlehem.

★ After Herod's death in 4 BC, the family returned and settled in Nazareth.

What the Bible doesn't say

★ The Bible doesn't say there were three wise men. Because three gifts are mentioned, people have imagined there must have been three men.

★ The visitors are not called kings. It is much more likely that they were astrologers — men who studied the stars for signs of important events on earth.

★ Over the years the 'three kings' have been given names which do not appear in the Bible: Melchior, Caspar and Balthazar.

★ Beautiful boxes and jars on cushions do not appear in the Bible, but the gifts were valuable.
  Frankincense was resin, collected from the bark of a tree. When burned, it gave off a sweet-scented smoke. It was used as incense in worship.
  Myrrh was also a resin, used as a spice, as a medicine and in preparing bodies for burial.

CHECK THE FACTS

You will find the Christmas story in the first two chapters of Matthew and Luke.

When a baby was born

Jewish people have always loved children. A big family was a sign of God's blessing. Boys were most valued because they could carry on the family name. Girls were thought to be less important, but were still loved and welcomed.

A new-born baby was washed and rubbed with salt. This was meant to make the skin firm. Then it was wrapped in 'swaddling cloths'. The mother laid the baby on a square of cloth and folded the corners over its sides and feet. Then long

The birth of Jesus (from the film, *Jesus of Nazareth*) was very different from most Christmas card pictures.

★ It doesn't actually say that Jesus was born in a stable. This idea comes from the fact that a manger, or animal feeding-trough, was used as a cot. It was usual for the animals to be housed on the ground floor of a house and for the family to live above, or in a raised part of the same room. An inn would also have plenty of room for visitors' animals.

★ There is no mention of the shepherds bringing baby lambs or any other presents to the baby.

★ The Bible does not mention snow (though snow can fall in this part of Israel in winter).

★ The innkeeper and his wife, stars of many nativity plays, are not mentioned in the Gospels. People imagine they must have been there because the Bible says there was an inn which was full!

bandages were wrapped round the whole bundle to keep the baby's arms straight by its sides. This made it easy for the mother to carry her baby in a woollen 'cradle' on her back.

The bandages were loosened several times a day and the baby's skin rubbed with olive oil and dusted with powdered myrtle leaves. This went on for several months.

Babies were normally breast-fed for two or three years.

Babies at the time of Jesus were tightly wrapped, like this.

Eight days after his birth, a baby boy was named. At the same time he was circumcised (the loose skin was cut off the top of his penis). This custom went back to the time of Abraham. It marked every man in Israel as one of God's own people.

If the child was the first boy in the family, he belonged to God in a special way. The family had to pay five pieces of silver to 'redeem' or buy him back.

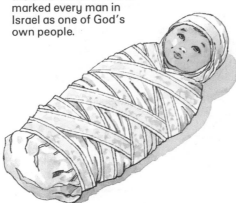

PREDICTIONS FOR THE BABY

An angel (speaking to Mary)
'. . . you will name him Jesus. He will be great and will be called the Son of the Most High God. The Lord God will make him a king, as his ancestor David was, and he will be the king of the descendants of Jacob for ever; his kingdom will never end!'

Simeon
'. . . with my own eyes I have seen your salvation, which you have prepared in the presence of all peoples: a light to reveal your will to the Gentiles and bring glory to your people Israel.'

Simeon (speaking to Mary)
'This child is chosen by God for the destruction and the salvation of many in Israel. He will be a sign from God which many people will speak against and so reveal their secret thoughts. And sorrow, like a sharp sword, will break your own heart.'

THE WAITING WORLD

For nearly 600 years before Jesus was born, Palestine, the land of the Jewish people, was under foreign rule. At the end of the Old Testament period there were the Babylonians and Persians. In the time between the Old and New Testaments, four more ruling powers held the land. The Jews governed themselves for only one brief spell of eighty years.

Countdown to Jesus

5 The Greeks
In 332 BC Alexander the Great took Palestine into the Greek Empire. Some Jews adopted the Greek way of life, giving their children Greek names and learning to speak the language.

4 The Ptolemies (Greek rulers of Egypt)
Nine years later, Alexander died and the empire was divided among his generals. General Ptolemy became the ruler of Egypt and his lands included Palestine. He did not interfere with Jewish life or religion.

3 The Seleucids (Greek rulers of Syria)
Another of Alexander's generals, Seleucus became the ruler of Syria. The kings of his line conquered the Ptolemies. In 198 BC they took control of Palestine. Antiochus IV, a later king, proved harsh and cruel. Many loyal Jews suffered under his rule. He went so far as to place a pagan altar in the temple at Jerusalem — and in 167 BC the Jews revolted.

2 Jewish freedom
The Jewish revolt against the Seleucids was led by Judas, Jonathan and Simon, the three sons of a priest. After three years of fighting, during which Judas became known as 'Maccabaeus' (the hammerer), the family managed to gain control of their own country. They were known as the Maccabees or Hasmoneans.

1 Roman (Italian) rule
The Hasmoneans were bad rulers, always fighting among themselves. In 63 BC the Roman general, Pompey, took advantage of this and claimed Judea for Rome. Later, a half-Jewish king, Herod the Great, was allowed to rule the country. Herod was king at the time when Jesus was born.

Greek language
Everywhere the Greek armies went, they spread Greek thought and culture. Greek became an international language and Greek ideas, Greek art, architecture and theatre had a very great influence on the world.

Roman peace
For over 500 years ordinary people had suffered as the great empires fought for control. They were tired of war and wanted to be able to live their lives in peace. Under Augustus Caesar, Rome was at last able to bring about some kind of peace.

The Romans made good roads, so that people could trade and travel more safely. They built baths,

meeting-houses and games stadiums. Everywhere they went, Roman soldiers kept order.

Greek and Roman religious ideas
Early in their history, the Greeks had many local gods. Gradually twelve gods became more important than the rest. Zeus, the all-wise protector of Greece, was their leader.

The Romans had the same number of gods, and gave them Roman names. Zeus, for instance, was called Jupiter.

As time passed, fewer and fewer people took these gods seriously. They began to search for someone or something to believe in, that would help them understand the world better.

The right time
By the end of the first century BC many ordinary Roman citizens were looking for something new to believe in — something to live for.

Roman roads, Roman peace and the fact that most people could speak Greek meant that ideas could spread fast.

The world was ready and waiting for the arrival of a very special person.

TEMPLE AND SYNAGOGUE

Jewish worship still focused on the temple in Jerusalem served by the priests, the place where God was especially close to his people. There the great festivals were celebrated, with thousands of pilgrims from all over the country coming to bring their sacrifices.

Some festival days reminded them of great events in their history. Others celebrated farming seasons such as Firstfruits and Harvest.

The inner room of the temple (the 'holy of holies') was so sacred that only one man — the high priest — was allowed in, just once a year on the Day of Atonement. This was the day when the whole nation confessed their sin and asked for God's forgiveness and a new start.

An animal was offered in sacrifice for their sins and its blood sprinkled in the 'holy of holies'.

Then the priest took a goat, known as the 'scapegoat', put his hand on its head and sent it away into the desert, as a sign that God had taken their sins away.

The temple was in constant use. Priests recited from the scriptures, said prayers, and led the morning and evening sacrifices every day. It was a place to hear the religious teachers, and people came there for special ceremonies such as the dedication of a new baby.

There was only one temple, but every town had its synagogue. Here people met together on the sabbath (Saturday — the day when all work stopped) for prayer and teaching. It was also the 'schoolhouse', where boys were taught by the rabbi, and the place of local government.

The Jewish world

By 40 BC the Romans were firmly in control of the country they called Palestine. They made Herod the Great king in 37 BC and kept an eye on things from Rome. Then in 4 BC Herod died and the kingdom was divided into three. Galilee in the north went to his son Herod Antipas and Judea (including Jerusalem) in the south went to another son, Archelaus.

Archelaus was such a harsh ruler that in AD 6 the Romans had to bring in a Governor (or Procurator) to take over Judea. From AD 26–36 the Governor was Pontius Pilate.

The Romans usually allowed a conquered people to continue with their own religion. So the Jews had their own religious authorities, based in Jerusalem. The High Priest and the main council, called the Sanhedrin, had control over all religious matters. They could punish people who had done wrong, but they were not allowed to put anyone to death.

Religious groups

The Pharisees were the strictest Jews, who tried to keep every part of the Law written in the Old Testament. Most of the 'scribes' (educated people who could write) were Pharisees. So too were the lawyers, who taught people the Law and explained its meaning.

The Sadducees were a smaller group of upper-class Jewish leaders, mostly members of the families of priests, who took a less strict approach to the Law than the Pharisees. The Sadducees had to be friendly towards the Romans, to keep their position. They were therefore mistrusted by most other Jews and unpopular with the ordinary people because of the profit they made from the temple market.

The small group of **Essenes** was even stricter than the Pharisees. Many of them lived in groups (rather like monks) out in the desert. They tried to keep the Jewish religion pure and free from outside influences. The most famous Essene community was at Qumran by the Dead Sea.

The Zealots were the nationalists, who hated the Romans. They formed themselves into small bands of freedom-fighters, dedicated to ridding the country of the foreign power. Their ambition was to return to the days when God ruled Israel — to bring in 'the kingdom of God'.

The Messiah

The one great hope of most Jewish people at this time was that God's promised Messiah would come.

'Messiah' means 'anointed one'. (In the Old Testament, kings, prophets and priests were anointed with oil as a sign of their appointment to special work.)

There were many predictions about the Messiah in their scriptures, and many Jews believed that he would be a great general, rather like their greatest king, David. But he would also be a priest-king, able to bring back the true worship of God. Under this king, who would rule in peace and justice, Israel would become a great nation once more.

No wonder people were longing for the Messiah to come!

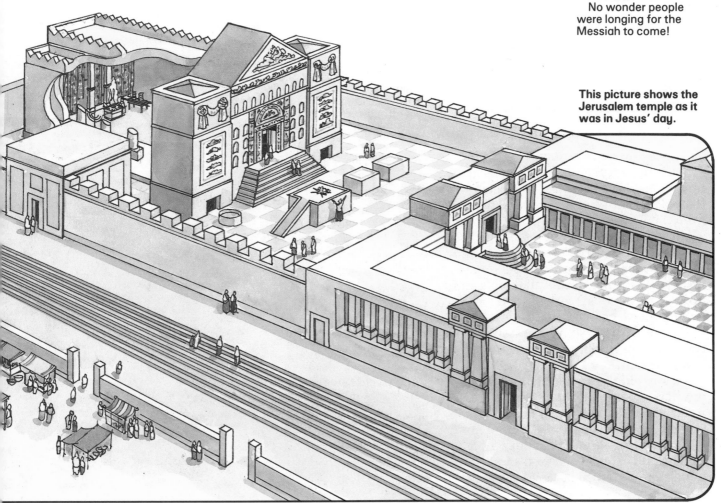

This picture shows the Jerusalem temple as it was in Jesus' day.

THE YEARS IN NAZARETH

Why don't we know anything about Jesus' life for the first thirty years?

Well, those who wrote his story down were keen to tell people the important bits about his life and these all happened in the last three years.

The last three years! His life was practically over by then.

Yes, but that's all the time he needed to do what he'd come to do.

Well, I still think it's strange that we don't know very much at all about someone who's supposed to be so important.

But we do. We know a surprising lot if you piece it all together.

What we know from the Gospels

The family lived in Nazareth, which was a busy town in Galilee, northern Palestine. Jesus grew up like any normal boy. Luke says he also grew in wisdom, gaining favour with God and all who knew him.

We are told he went regularly to the synagogue every sabbath. When he grew up he must have been well respected there. He was one of those called to read from the Law.

His father Joseph was a joiner or carpenter. In those days carpenters were often builders too, working from home, making furniture, agricultural tools and doing any practical work needed locally. It would have been normal for Jesus to be in the family firm, so we can assume he was a skilled workman and a good businessman.

We are told the names of four of Jesus' brothers — James, Joseph, Simon and Judas. And Matthew mentions 'all his sisters' as well. The words 'brother' and 'sister' can sometimes be more generally understood as 'relative'. And a tradition which can be traced back at least to the third century says that Jesus' mother Mary had no other children and that these were Jesus' cousins. This is the view of the Roman Catholic church.

Luke gives a detailed description of one incident from Jesus' childhood which tells us a lot about him. It was the time the family took him up to Jerusalem for the Passover Festival. Jesus was twelve years old.

Joseph and Mary had gone a whole day on the return journey, when they realized Jesus was not with them. They rushed back and found him in the temple, talking with the religious teachers. Luke says they were all 'amazed at his intelligent answers'.

Understandably, his parents told him off for causing them so much worry. But Jesus said, 'Didn't you know that I had to be in my Father's house?' — an answer that completely confused them. It shows that, even at twelve, Jesus was already aware of God as his Father in a special way.

What we know about everyday life

His home

A typical small family house of Jesus' day (shown in the picture) was made from wood and sun-baked mud. The family lived upstairs and made use of the flat roof as an extra room. Work would be carried on downstairs and the animals were kept there too. Poor families had only the downstairs room, with a higher level for the living area.

Education

The local synagogue was an important focus in the village. As well as the meeting-place for sabbath services, it doubled as the school.

There, boys between the ages of five and thirteen were taught by the rabbi or religious teacher.

Each boy had to learn portions of the Old Testament by heart, because the main aim of education was to make him a good Jew who understood the scriptures.

Joseph teaches Jesus carpentry; from the film, *Jesus of Nazareth*.

THE COUNTRY JESUS LOVED

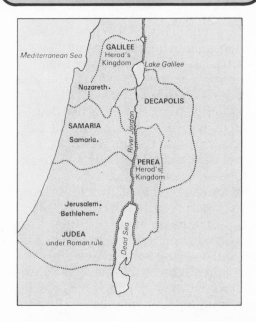

Coming of age

On his thirteenth birthday a Jewish boy was regarded as an adult. This was marked by a service called the Bar Mitzvah (son of the Law), at which he had to recite the scripture readings. The rabbi then said a special prayer of blessing for him.

Look up the details about Jesus' childhood; Nazareth: Luke 2:39; Sabbath: Luke 4:16; Carpenter, brothers and sisters: Mark 6:1–3; Jerusalem: Luke 2:41–52.

The land where Jesus lived was called Palestine by the Romans. Today most of it is in Israel.

It is not very big — less than 230 km/143 miles long (and about the area of Wales). But within this small land the countryside changes from sandy desert to green plains, from Mt Hermon in the north at nearly 3,000 m /9,000 ft to the Dead Sea which is the lowest point on earth, 388 m /1,270 ft below sea level.

This varied countryside can be strikingly beautiful. It is rich in all kinds of plant, animal and bird life, too. In Jesus' day much more of the land was covered with thick forest and there were wild bears, foxes, jackals and even leopards.

This is the kind of house an ordinary family lived in at the time of Jesus.

Lake Galilee and the towns around its shores became the base for most of Jesus' work. With friends in the fishing trade, he could cross the lake by boat whenever he wanted.

THE WORK BEGINS

Jesus was about thirty years old when he left home to begin his special work.

The first thing he did was to travel the 100 km/62 miles from Nazareth to Bethany on the east side of the River Jordan, where his cousin John was preaching and baptizing people.

Jesus asked John to baptize him.

John was shocked. He knew that Jesus had done nothing wrong and did not need forgiveness. But Jesus insisted. His baptism was to be the sign that he had begun his work, that he was willing to follow God wholeheartedly and do all that he required.

So John agreed to baptize Jesus. 'As soon as Jesus was baptized,' Matthew says, 'he came up out of the water. Then heaven was opened to him, and he saw the Spirit of God coming down like a dove and alighting on him. Then a voice said from heaven, ''This is my own dear Son, with whom I am pleased.'''
Matthew 3:16–17

Today, Christians in some churches are still baptized by being dipped completely under the water, as Jesus would have been.

Baptism is a kind of picture — it shows the person being washed clean of all the wrong things he or she has done in the past, and coming up again to a new start.

It is rather like dying, and coming to life again.

Cousin John

John the Baptist was the son of a priest called Zechariah. His wife Elizabeth was related to Mary, Jesus' mother.

When John was born, an angel told his father that he would be special:

'. . . He will go ahead of the Lord, strong and mighty like the prophet Elijah . . . he will get the Lord's people ready for him.'

When John grew up, he left home for a lonely life in the Judean Desert, eating only the food that could be found there.

He dressed in rough camel-hair clothes and was everybody's idea of a holy man.

Crowds came out to hear him preach. 'Turn away from your sins — all that you've done wrong,' he said. 'And be baptized — washed clean.'

Those who were prepared to change their ways were baptized in the River Jordan as a sign that God had forgiven them.

CHECK THE FACTS

You can find the story of John's life and work in Luke's Gospel chapters 1, 3 and 7 and his death in Mark 6.

In the Judean Desert John the Baptist preached and Jesus fasted for forty days, facing decisions about his work.

A hard test

Immediately after the excitement of his baptism, Jesus faced one of his hardest tests. He went away by himself into the dry Judean Desert to pray and to think about the work he must do and how to carry it out.

He was there for 'forty days and nights', the Gospel writers say, and during that time he ate nothing.

Then, we are told, the Devil — God's age-old enemy — came to tempt Jesus. We don't know if he actually appeared to Jesus in some way, or whether Jesus simply had to fight the temptation to do things for the wrong reasons. But the temptations themselves are very clear.

1

'If you are God's Son,' came the tempting voice, 'order this stone to turn into bread.'

Should Jesus use his power to satisfy his own hunger or to feed people? Food is necessary. It would satisfy them for a while, but would that be enough?

Jesus' reply came from the Old Testament book of Deuteronomy:

'The scripture says, ''Man cannot live on bread alone, but needs every word that God speaks.'''

2

Then the Devil took Jesus to the highest point of the temple at Jerusalem. 'If you are God's Son,' he taunted, 'throw yourself down, for the scripture says, ''God will give orders to his angels about you; they will hold you up with their hands, so that not even your feet will be hurt on the stones.'''

These words are from Psalm 91. The Devil was trying to persuade Jesus to do something spectacular that would draw the crowds.

Jesus firmly rejected this method of gaining followers. 'But the scripture also says, ''Do not put the Lord your God to the test,''' came his answer.

Alone in the desert, hungry and thirsty, Jesus faced some hard testing.

3

Then Jesus was taken to a high mountain and was shown all the kingdoms of the world. 'All this I will give you, if you kneel down and worship me,' he was told.

Jesus knew he was being offered an easy way to get power. He replied without hesitation: 'Go away, Satan! The scripture says, ''Worship the Lord your God and serve only him!'''

CHECK THE FACTS

You can find Jesus' conversation with the Devil in Matthew chapter 4.

DISCIPLES AND FRIENDS

You can learn a great deal about a person from the kind of friends he makes — and Jesus was no exception.

Jesus was friends with all kinds of different people. In fact, he shocked the people of his day because he chose friends they thought were unsuitable for a religious teacher. But Jesus took no notice of their opinions.

He was happy to be friends with people who had no money, and with those the Pharisees called 'sinners'. He had friends among the wealthy and powerful too.

Crowds of people followed Jesus wherever he went. Many wanted him to heal or help them in some way; others to hear him teach and listen to his stories.

From this large group, Jesus chose twelve men as his special disciples or followers (the word means 'student' or 'pupil'). They were to be with him all the time.

Even in choosing these men, Jesus did not play safe. Simon the Zealot (or Patriot) hated the Romans; Matthew had been a tax collector, working for them! There must have been a few arguments between those two, but somehow following Jesus brought them together.

The film *Jesus of Nazareth* shows Jesus walking along the quayside by Lake Galilee. Peter and Andrew, James and John were busy with their nets when Jesus called them to follow him.

The Twelve

Peter (Simon) was a partner in a fishing business in Galilee. He was married. He had a fiery temper but his strong personality, and later his strong faith, made him a leader among the disciples.

Andrew was Peter's brother and partner, but he had left his work to become a follower of John the Baptist. When Jesus came to be baptized, Andrew joined him.

James and **John** were fishermen in business with their father. They were so hot-headed that Jesus nicknamed them 'sons of thunder'! John was probably Jesus' closest friend. When Jesus died, John looked after his mother Mary.

Philip came from Bethsaida, a town on the edge of Lake Galilee. He was one of the first disciples to follow Jesus.

Nathanael (Bartholomew) was a friend of Philip. Jesus described him as a 'real Israelite — with nothing false in him'.

Matthew (Levi) was a tax collector. The job would have made him a lot of money, but no friends among his own people. It meant working for the Romans.

Simon belonged to the Zealots, a political group working to get rid of the Romans.

Thomas was later nicknamed 'the doubter', because he refused to believe that Jesus had risen from death until he had seen him and touched his scars. In fact, he was a brave and faithful disciple.

James was known as 'son of Alphaeus' to avoid confusion with John's brother James.

Judas Thaddeus was known as 'son of James'.

Judas Iscariot's surname may mean 'from Kerioth'. If so, he was the only southerner among the disciples. But the name can also mean 'dagger man'. He was treasurer of the group and the others suspected him of taking money from the purse for his own use. Finally he betrayed Jesus to the religious authorities. Afterwards he regretted it and committed suicide.

Other friends

Mary, Martha and Lazarus lived at Bethany, outside Jerusalem, and Jesus loved to visit their home. The two sisters were very different from each other. On one occasion, when Jesus was at their house for a meal, Martha complained that Mary was listening to Jesus talking and not helping to get the meal ready. Jesus told her to stop worrying about all she had to do. Listening was important too!

Joanna and **Susanna** were among a group of wealthy women who went around with Jesus and the disciples, looking after them. Joanna's husband Chuza was an officer in King Herod's court.

Mary Magdalene is described as having been freed by Jesus from 'seven evil spirits'. (This may have been some kind of demon possession, or perhaps a severe mental illness.) She became one of Jesus' closest friends.

JESUS' TEACHING: ABOUT GOD

After his baptism, Jesus left home and began work going from place to place as a teacher. His message was simple and direct. He called people to put God first in their lives. He showed them how to please God, how to live happy lives and how to treat each other. He spoke so clearly and with such certainty that people were amazed.

As soon as word went round that the new teacher was coming to their town, people flocked to hear him. It must have been like being a pop star today. Several times Jesus was nearly mobbed. Once he had to climb into a boat and speak from a little way out on the lake so that people could hear him!

'The people who heard him were amazed at the way he taught . . .'
Mark 1:22

'The large crowd listened to him with delight.'
Mark 12:37

Jesus teaches in the temple; from the film, *Jesus of Nazareth*.

WHERE GOD RULES

Jesus told the crowds that he had come to give them some good news. The kingdom of God (he sometimes called it the kingdom of heaven) had come.

A kingdom is all the land and all the people ruled by a single king — even when they go out of the country.

When Jesus announced the beginning of God's kingdom he was talking about a people, rather than a country. Everyone prepared to accept God as king in his or her life can belong to God's kingdom, no matter who they are or where they live.

Jesus used examples from everyday life to explain how the kingdom would come.

Yeast
The kingdom of heaven is like a spoonful of yeast that you put into the bread mix. It bubbles away inside the dough and, very soon, the whole loaf is light and delicious. All because of that little bit of yeast.

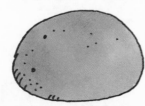

So the number of people who have God as their king is growing all the time, spreading quietly throughout the world, like the yeast in the dough.

Pearl
The kingdom of heaven is like a really valuable pearl, hidden in an oyster shell. When a pearl collector opens the shell and sees it, he knows it is worth more than his whole collection of pearls put together. He wants it so much that he sells everything he has to own it.

So, to belong to God's kingdom is the most important thing in the world. It is worth giving up everything else for.

Seed
The kingdom of heaven is like a tiny mustard seed. It's just a little black dot. But, take the little black dot and plant it — and what happens? It grows!

At first it grows quietly in the dark earth. No one can see a thing. Then a green

A Roman soldier came to Jesus to beg him to cure his servant who was ill. Jesus was impressed with the officer's faith and healed the servant.

Mothers and children crowded around Jesus wherever he went. Unlike many busy people, he had time for them, and a special love for children.

Simon the Pharisee invited Jesus to dinner in his house. Jesus was happy to go, even though he often told the Pharisees off because of their proud ways.

Joseph of Arimathea and **Nicodemus** were both members of the ruling Jewish Council — the Sanhedrin. They were secret followers of Jesus. But when he was crucified Joseph offered the use of the tomb he owned and Nicodemus brought spices to prepare the body for burial.

WHAT DO YOU THINK?

Do people have disciples today? Can you think of any examples?

What is God like?

Jesus did not change any of the basic things the Jews believed about God. In fact, he emphasized them and made them clearer.

These are the main ideas about God that come from the Old Testament:

★ God is the creator of the universe. He existed before anything was made, outside time and space. He is the power that keeps the whole universe going.

★ He is holy. That means he is totally good and pure. There is no evil or bad side to him at all.

★ He is always fair and just. He knows what goes on in the world and one day he will put things right, so that goodness is rewarded and those who do wrong are punished.

★ He is a God of love. He cares about the things he has made. He especially loves people, even though many of them do not believe in him and some have chosen to be his enemies.

shoot appears, a stem, leaves, branches. Finally, standing there, where you planted the little black seed, is a plant like a small tree. Birds can nest in it. It is a beautiful thing.

Today the small 'seed' Jesus planted — the little group of his followers — has grown to become a world-wide 'church' of his people.

CHECK THE FACTS

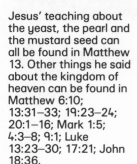

Jesus' teaching about the yeast, the pearl and the mustard seed can all be found in Matthew 13. Other things he said about the kingdom of heaven can be found in Matthew 6:10; 13:31–33; 19:23–24; 20:1–16; Mark 1:5; 4:3–8; 9:1; Luke 13:23–30; 17:21; John 18:36.

THE LOST SON

Jesus liked to talk about God as a perfect, loving father who cares about people and wants them to be part of his family, or his kingdom. One of his best-known stories shows this clearly:

THERE WAS ONCE a man who had two sons. The elder boy helped his father with the house and the farm. But the younger one was bored and fed up.

One day the younger son said to his father, 'I'm leaving. I want to live my own life and enjoy myself. Give me my share of the farm now.'

So his father divided up his land. He gave half to the younger boy, who promptly sold it, took the money and left.

He went abroad, spending the money like water. He had a beautiful house, clothes, food and lots of friends. Until the money ran out. Then he had to sell everything, bit by bit. And of course the friends left too.

Worse followed. There was a poor harvest and very few people had food. Those with no money starved.

The boy managed to get a job — the lowest kind there was in that country — minding pigs. He got so hungry he was even picking bits out of the pigs' food!

'This is crazy!' he said to himself. 'At home, even the servants are eating well, while I starve. After what I've done, I can't expect a welcome. But I could get work on the farm.' So he set off.

As he came near his old home, the boy was amazed to see someone, who had been standing by the gate, running towards him down the road. It was his father!

The next moment they were hugging and kissing one another.

Then the boy stepped back and took a deep breath. He had to say the words he had been preparing every step of the way home.

'Father, I have been in the wrong. I've let God — and you — down. I know I can't come back as your son. But would you take me on as one of your workmen?'

His father didn't seem to have heard him. 'Off with those rags!' he ordered the servants. 'Here, put on this robe. And shoes, and a ring for his finger. Then run and kill one of the calves. We shall have a great party tonight. I thought my son was dead, but here he is alive. I have found my own son again!'

God is as loving as that father, said Jesus, always ready to forgive people who are really sorry for what they have done wrong.

It doesn't matter whether a person has always loved God, like the older brother in the story, or has been a rebel, like the younger one. Jesus' story is intended to show that anyone can belong to God's kingdom and be welcomed into his family. And that's good news!

CHECK THE FACTS

This story and two others, the lost sheep and the lost coin, come from Luke 15.

JESUS AND PRAYER

Jesus' disciples asked him to teach them to pray, because they could see how important prayer was in his own life.

Jesus had very little time to himself. From early morning till late at night he was surrounded by people wanting him to help them. Yet, by getting up very early in the morning, and going out into the countryside by himself, Jesus still managed to find time to be alone with God.

Of course, praying to God was not a new idea for the disciples. The Old Testament, particularly the Psalms, is full of examples of people thanking God for things, or bringing their problems to him. At home, every Jew was expected to pray three times a day. Some Pharisees made a great show of saying their prayers in a public place.

So when Jesus talked about prayer, he was not teaching something new. But his approach to prayer was different, and people found it surprising.

Jesus spends time with his disciples; from the film, *Jesus of Nazareth.*

HOW TO PRAY

● Jesus taught that we can call God 'Father'. (The word Jesus used was more like our word 'Daddy'.) He encouraged people to think of God as their loving father — someone who knew just what they needed before they asked. 'He even knows the exact number of hairs on your head!' Jesus told them.

● Prayer is a private conversation. Prayers don't have to be long and impressive to be heard. Prayer is not something to show off about. 'When you pray,' Jesus told his disciples, 'go to your room, close the door, and pray to your Father, who is unseen. And your Father, who sees what you do in private, will reward you.'

● Jesus taught that anyone who prays can be absolutely sure that God hears and will answer in the way that is best for them. If he seems slow in answering, keep on praying and trusting God.

● The attitude of the person praying is important. It's no good coming to God to ask him to forgive you, Jesus said, if you won't forgive your own family and friends!

People can talk to God (pray) at any time and anywhere.

CHECK THE FACTS

Jesus' teaching on how to pray comes in Matthew 6:5–15; 7:7–11; 18:19–20; 26:41; Mark 11:22–26; Luke 11:1–13; 18:1–14.

The Lord's Prayer

Jesus was always practical. When his disciples asked him to teach them to pray, he gave them an actual prayer to say. You will find the words in Matthew 6:9–13 and Luke 11:2–4.

'Our Father in heaven,
May your name be kept holy;
may your Kingdom come;
may your will be done
on earth as it is in heaven.
Give us today the food we need.
Forgive us the wrongs we have done,
as we forgive the wrongs
that others have done to us.
Do not bring us to hard testing,
but keep us safe from the Evil One.'

The different translations have slightly different words (you may want to compare them), but when they pray this prayer, people are:

★ worshipping God, thinking about who he is and how great he is

★ declaring that they are on his side, part of his kingdom

★ asking for his help with their daily needs

★ confessing that they have done wrong things and promising to forgive others

★ asking for protection and strength

PRAYER TODAY

Many people today can tell of practical answers to their prayers. Here are two examples.

Martin Luther King remembers a point during his fight for equal rights for black people in the USA, when he felt he could not go on.

'In this state of exhaustion, when my courage had almost gone, I determined to take my problem to God.

'My head in my hands, I bowed over the kitchen table and prayed aloud. The words I spoke to God that midnight are still vivid in my memory. "I am here taking a stand for what I believe is right. But now I am afraid. The people are looking to me for leadership, and if I stand before them without strength and courage they too will falter. I am at the end of my powers. I have nothing left. I've come to the point where I can't face it alone."

'At that moment I experienced the presence of God as I had never before experienced him. It seemed as though I could hear the quiet assurance of an inner voice, saying, "Stand up for righteousness, stand up for truth. God will be at your side for ever."

'Almost at once my fears began to pass from me. My uncertainty disappeared. I was ready to face anything. The outer situation remained the same, but God had given me inner calm.'

Delia Smith, cookery writer and television presenter, remembers:

'I have always prayed — it began with my mother giving me a picture of Jesus when I was three years old. She taught me to pray every night, and through my life my prayer-life has grown.

'I think it's important to bring God into the whole of our lives, asking him to help us throughout each day and in every situation. I also think prayers of thanksgiving are important, and spending some quiet time reading the Bible.

'You can't love God unless you know him and you can only know him by reading about him and praying to him.

'I pray before going on television. I find that if I feel anxious or nervous about something like a television recording, putting the whole thing in God's hands does really help . . .

WHAT DO YOU THINK?

Why do you think God sometimes seems to be answering 'No' when we pray for things?

When Jesus was asked to say which was the most important rule to follow in the Old Testament, he quoted Deuteronomy 6:5: 'Love the Lord your God with all your heart, with all your soul, and with all your strength.'

But he followed it up with a second quotation, from Leviticus 19:18, which says God's people must love others 'as they love themselves'.

The rabbis had always taught that this meant Jews should love and care for their own countrymen. But when a scribe asked what the commandment really meant, Jesus took it a stage further by telling them a story:

THE GOOD SAMARITAN

THERE WAS ONCE a man who was on his way from Jerusalem to Jericho. Suddenly, robbers attacked him, stripped him and beat him up, leaving him half dead.

It so happened that a priest was going down the same road. When he saw the man lying there, he crossed over to the other side of the road and hurried past.

A Levite (someone who helped the priests in the temple) came by next. He went over and looked at the man. But then he also crossed over and continued his journey.

But a Samaritan (a man from Samaria, considered a foreigner by the Jews) was going that way. When he saw the man, he was instantly sorry for him. He went over to him, attended to his wounds and bandaged them up. Then he put the man on his own donkey and took him to an inn.

The next day he had to leave, so he gave the innkeeper two silver coins and said, 'Take care of him and when I come back this way, I will pay you whatever else you spend on him.'
Luke 10:30–35

The scribes were surprised and shocked by this story. Samaritans were foreigners and old enemies. They refused to worship God at the temple in Jerusalem.

Anyone, even the youngest, can care for others, as Jesus taught.

Yet here was Jesus, saying that it was the Samaritan who obeyed God's rule about caring for others. He even seemed to suggest that to look after someone in need was more important than religious duties.

This is typical of Jesus' attitude to others. The rest of his teaching can be summed up like this:

★ God knows and cares about each individual, even down to the number of hairs on a person's head!

★ Every person is equal in God's sight. Jesus taught this by example, making friends with all kinds of people — men and women, rich and poor, Jews and non-Jews.

★ Everyone does wrong and displeases God. But people can repent, or turn back from the things they do wrong, and return to God. He is always ready to forgive. People must be prepared to forgive one another too.

★ God expects those who belong to his kingdom to care for others in a practical way.

CARING TODAY, FOR JESUS' SAKE

In 1964 **Jean Vanier** founded the first L'Arche (the ark) Community in France, where people who are mentally handicapped can live together with others as equals. His ideas spring from Jesus' example in caring particularly for those who are pushed to one side and neglected in our world.

In Britain **Cicely Saunders** helped to found the hospice movement, providing especially equipped hospitals for people who are dying. As a Christian, she believes that people should have the right to be looked after by those who can help them to understand death and face it with dignity.

Many Christian organizations — **Christian Aid, CAFOD, Compassion, World Vision, TEAR Fund** and countless others — are

THE SERMON ON THE MOUNT

at work all over the world, bringing emergency help where disasters have struck. They also provide money, given by ordinary Christians, for long-term projects such as wells for clean water, seed for crops, hospitals, schools and training schemes.

In 1974 one of the American President's advisors, **Charles Colson**, was sent to prison for his part in the illegal activities which became known as the 'Watergate' affair.

Just before this happened, Charles Colson became a Christian. During his time in prison, he discovered that many prisoners need help and advice but have no one to turn to.

When he returned to normal life, Colson decided to put Jesus' teaching into action. He gathered together a group of people willing to visit and help prisoners, and founded The Prison Christian Fellowship.

In chapters 5–7 of his Gospel, Matthew gives us a good example of the kind of things Jesus taught. (It is sometimes called the 'Sermon on the Mount' because Matthew records, 'Jesus saw the crowds and went up a hill, where he sat down. His disciples gathered around him, and he began to teach them.')

How to be happy

Most people think that, to be happy, you need to be tough, successful and pushy.

It's not like that at all, said Jesus. Sitting on the hillside, he gave his disciples this list of people who are truly happy:

'Happy are those who know they are spiritually poor;
The Kingdom of heaven belongs to them!
Happy are those who mourn;
God will comfort them!
Happy are those who are humble;
they will receive what God has promised!
Happy are those whose greatest desire is to do what God requires;
God will satisfy them fully!
Happy are those who are merciful to others;
God will be merciful to them!
Happy are the pure in heart;
they will see God!
Happy are those who work for peace;
God will call them his children!
Happy are those who are persecuted because they do what God requires;
The Kingdom of heaven belongs to them!'

(These statements are sometimes called the 'Beatitudes' because they begin, 'Blessed (or happy) are . . .')

According to Jesus, the people who will be truly happy are the humble, the forgiving, the pure, those who set their hearts on what is right, who try to be peacemakers — even those who are having a hard time because they have done what is right. They are really happy because they are in God's kingdom already.

In the rest of the 'sermon', Jesus showed that it is not enough to think that you can please God by keeping rules and laws. It is the attitude inside that counts. For instance, a person may not have killed anyone, but if he keeps on hating someone, that is just as bad.

Jesus covered a whole range of very practical things that everyone needs help with: anger, swearing, wanting to take revenge, marriage and divorce, how to deal with enemies, attitudes to money and possessions, criticizing others. And he talked about the good things to do — caring for people, giving to the poor, praying for people, standing up for what is right and above all wanting to serve and obey God.

Have you heard the one about the man who tried to take the speck of sawdust out of his brother's eye? He couldn't do it.

Why not?

He had a log in his own!

This comes from one of Jesus' short stories. Look it up in Matthew 7:1–5 and see what it means.

THE POWER TO MAKE PEOPLE WELL

One of the reasons why people flocked to see Jesus was that they knew he could cure those who were ill.

It's hard for us to imagine living in a time when there were no hospitals and very little medical care. There were literally thousands of people desperate for help.

The Gospels describe Jesus' remarkable power to heal. They tell how he cured all kinds of illness and handicap, how he opened blind eyes, freed people from the power of evil, and even brought them back to life — simply with a word.

But Jesus never did these things simply to attract followers. He decided against this right at the beginning of his work (see **5**). Most of the time he tried not to draw attention to this side of his work because it attracted crowds who just wanted to see something amazing happen.

Why did Jesus heal people?

This is what the Gospel writers tell us:

★ Jesus used his power because he loved people. He hated to see them in pain or trouble. The Gospels often say, '. . . Jesus' heart went out to them and he healed them.'

★ The wonderful things Jesus did were signs that what he said was true. If Jesus could do these amazing things that people could see, surely he could also do the thing that couldn't be seen, like forgiving wrongdoing and giving people a new start. People could see the powers of evil, illness and death being overcome.

★ Jesus' healing powers were a sign that he was the Messiah, the one sent by God whom the Jews were expecting. Isaiah, a prophet in the Old Testament, had predicted that the Messiah would heal people. So, when John the Baptist asked Jesus if he really *was* the Messiah, he pointed as proof to the things he was doing.

Sick people were brought to Jesus for healing; this man (from the film, Jesus of Nazareth) could not walk.

A man born blind

One day Jesus met a man who had been born blind. To help him, Jesus bent down and spat on the ground, making a kind of mud which he smeared on the man's eyes.

'Go and wash your face in the Pool of Siloam,' Jesus said. The man went, washed his face, and came back — able to see.

Those who knew him began to whisper, 'Isn't this the man who used to sit and beg?'

'No, it can't be. It just looks like him.'

The man himself spoke up, 'It is me.'

'How come you can see?' everyone wanted to know.

So the man told them the whole story, and they took him to the authorities, where he told his story once again.

The Pharisees were not impressed.

'He cured you on the sabbath day? That's not allowed!' they said. 'He can't come from God.'

Others disagreed.

'How can someone heal a man who was born blind, without God's power?'

The Pharisees asked the healed man, 'Who do you think he is?'

'He is a prophet sent by God,' he answered.

'Maybe he wasn't actually blind in the first place,' someone suggested. So they called his parents.

The man's mother and father were afraid to make the Pharisees angry.

'He was certainly born blind,' they said, 'but you'll have to ask him what happened. He's a grown man. He can speak for himself.'

The cross-examination continued, until finally the healed man lost patience.

'I don't know about your religious problems,' he exploded. 'All I know is that I was blind, and now I can see . . .'

When Jesus heard all this he went and found the man and asked gently, 'Do you believe in the Son of man?' (See **12**.)

'Tell me who he is sir, so that I can believe in him!' replied the man.

'You have already seen him, and he is the one who is talking with you now,' said Jesus.

'I believe, Lord!' said the man, kneeling down.

Then Jesus said something strange: 'I came to this world to judge, so that the blind should see and those who see should be as if they were blind.'

Read this story for yourself in John 9. What do you think Jesus meant by those last words?

PAGES FROM DR LUKE'S CASEBOOK

Luke, the author of the third Gospel and the book of Acts, was not one of the Twelve. He became a follower of Jesus later and helped the apostle Paul on his preaching and teaching journeys. But he made a careful study of all the events of Jesus' life, which he then recorded in his Gospel. It is generally believed that he was a doctor himself, so he would have had a special interest in Jesus' ability to heal people.

Perhaps Dr Luke made notes, something like these, on the cases he investigated.

Case 14

Adult, male

This man was suffering from acute swelling of the arms and legs, caused by excess fluid in the blood.

He approached Jesus when he was having a sabbath meal at the home of a leading Pharisee. Jesus took the man's hands, looked at him and cured the condition in front of the whole gathering. He then sent the man away because the Pharisees began to complain that such work should not be done on the sabbath.
Luke 14:1–6

More trouble!

Case 12

Adult, female.

This woman had suffered a crippling disease, which left her bent almost double. The condition was chronic and had lasted for some eighteen years. She attended the synagogue where Jesus was teaching on the sabbath. Jesus saw her and called out, 'Woman, you are free from your illness!' He then put his hand on her and she was instantly seen to straighten up. The woman was understandably delighted and full of praise to God.
Luke 13:10–17

This incident caused trouble for Jesus because it took place on the sabbath.

Case 15

Ten adults, male

Severe skin condition, possibly leprosy.

This group were outcasts, allowed to live only on the outskirts of a town on the borders of Samaria and Galilee. As Jesus approached they called out, 'Jesus! Master! Take pity on us!' He simply replied, 'Go and let the priests examine you.' When they reported to the authorities for a medical check, they were found to be completely free of the condition.
Luke 17:11–19

Only one of these men returned to thank Jesus. He was a Samaritan!

Healing today

Ever since the earliest days of the church, Christians have followed the example of Jesus in caring for the sick. Today there are many hospitals around the world, founded and run by Christians.

This Christian nurse helps to make the day interesting for a young patient in hospital.

JERUSALEM ✡ STAR

5,000 FED IN MIRACLE MEAL DRAMA

'He used my lunch,' says boy.

'Miracle Man' Jesus of Nazareth yesterday fed a crowd of 5,000 men, plus women and children, with one boy's lunch. In a feat that defies explanation, the one-time carpenter took five barley loaves and two fish and made supper for the lakeside gathering who had come to hear his teaching.

Jesus (30), who has been drawing thousands of working people to his off-the-cuff open-air preaching and healing sessions in recent months, worked this 'miracle' on the eastern shore of Lake Galilee yesterday evening.

Observers report that Jesus had set off from Capernaum by boat during the morning in a bid to escape the crowds who have followed him from town to town. But, so determined were they to hear his teaching, the throng pursued him around the lake on foot. They were waiting for him on the other side when he stepped ashore.

Miracle healings
In a now familiar pattern, Jesus spent much of his time with the disabled and the unwell, apparently bringing miraculous cures simply by the touch of his hand.

But Jesus has also gained a nationwide reputation as a teacher of exceptional gifts, who uses stories to get his point across. This huge crowd of men, women and children sat in rapt attention for hours as he taught his own brand of popular religion.

It was almost sunset when Jesus' small team of disciples suggested that the crowds might be sent home. Jesus appears to have asked what arrangements could be made for them to eat.

Philip, a close associate of the teacher, estimated that the food bill for the crowd would come to 200 silver coins.

Boy's offer
It was then that Andrew, another of Jesus' followers, was approached by a 12-year-old boy, who offered the disciple the loaves and fish he had brought for lunch and had not eaten.

What followed might not have been believed, even by this reporter, had it not been witnessed by so many. Jesus accepted the gift and asked the crowd to arrange themselves in groups of fifty and a hundred on the grass.

Food for all
Taking the bread and fish in his hands he said grace and began handing portions to his disciples for distribution. How this small meal multiplied itself so many thousands of times is beyond the understanding of even the closest observers. But the crowd ate their fill. In fact the portions were so generous that Jesus' followers were able to collect enough leftovers to fill twelve baskets.

Rumours
The events that followed were typically Galilean. Rumours began to circulate that this man was the Messiah. People jumped to their feet and a chant began in a move to proclaim the young preacher as king. Things could have become dangerous, but Jesus took advantage of the chaos to slip away. Last night he was unavailable for comment.

Water into wine

There was to be a wedding in the town of Cana in Galilee. Jesus' mother was there. Jesus and his disciples had also been invited.

Weddings were exciting affairs in those days. The feasting and entertainments often lasted for days.

Something went wrong with the arrangements at this particular wedding, however, because the wine ran out! The steward in charge of the feast was in a state about it. What a disgrace — no wine!

Without hesitating, Jesus' mother found Jesus and told him.

'What is it to do with me?' asked Jesus. (He did not want to use his special powers just to impress people.)

'Do whatever he says,' Mary said to the servants. They turned and looked at Jesus.

There were six large water jars standing nearby. 'Fill them up with water,' said Jesus.

When they had done so, he said, 'Now pour out some of the water and take it to the man in charge.'

Somewhere between the water jar and the wine taster, something remarkable happened.

'Who's been hanging on to the best wine?' the steward asked the bridegroom. The servants smiled at Jesus. They were the only ones who knew the truth.

Read this story for yourself in John chapter 2.

As well as Jesus' healings, the Gospels recount other remarkable events. They involve the power to set aside the usual laws of nature for a special reason.

Jesus knew that such powers, just like the ability to heal people, could easily be used to draw crowds and impress them. He was careful to use them only amongst his friends, or in exceptional circumstances to help others.

Jesus' special powers were very far-reaching:

★ **Power over the forces of nature.** When a violent storm blew up as they were crossing Lake Galilee, the disciples woke Jesus because they were terrified. Jesus calmed the storm with a command. On another occasion he walked over the lake and joined his friends in their boat. Then he made it possible for Peter to walk briefly across the water as well.

★ **Power over everyday objects.** Twice Jesus is recorded as having fed great crowds from a small amount of food, and at Cana he turned a large quantity of water into wine. He also told the fishermen where to fish, so that they made their biggest catch ever.

★ **Power over death itself.** On three occasions Jesus was able to bring people back to life after they had died. The last of these was his friend Lazarus, who had been dead and buried for four days.

The amazing things Jesus did produced very mixed reactions from the people who saw them.

Jesus' close friends were encouraged by seeing glimpses of his true power. It helped them to have faith in him when things got tough. But they were also rather frightened by it. Once, when Jesus helped Peter make a huge catch of fish, Peter threw himself at Jesus' feet and said, 'Leave me, Lord! I am a sinful man!'

The religious leaders, on the other hand, could not admit that Jesus' power came from God. To do so would have been to agree that he was right and they were wrong. They decided that Jesus must be in touch with evil forces and he must be stopped.

WHERE TO FIND JESUS' PARABLES

WHERE TO FIND JESUS' HEALINGS

WHERE TO FIND JESUS' MIRACLES

Note: many of these events are recorded in more than one Gospel

Names were very important to the Jewish people. Jesus was known by several different names and titles and each one gave part of the picture of the special person he claimed to be.

The rescuer

His own name — Jesus — given to him by the angel who appeared to Mary in Nazareth, was another form of the name Joshua. It meant 'rescuer'. Jesus told several stories to show that he had come 'to seek and save the lost'. The Good Shepherd is the best known.

THERE WAS ONCE a shepherd who had 100 sheep. He knew every one of them by name, as all good shepherds should.

One evening he was counting them back into the fold for the night, when he noticed that one was missing. One, out of 100! What did he do?

He went straight back to look for the lost sheep.

When he finally found it, he was so happy, he picked it up and carried it all the way home on his shoulders.

He was still happy when he got home. So pleased, in fact, that he called everyone in for a celebration party.

'I tell you,' said Jesus, 'God is as happy as that shepherd, when even one person says he is sorry for going his own way, comes back to God and is ''found''.'
Luke 15:1–7

A good shepherd takes great care of his sheep. This is a modern-day picture, taken in Israel.

The Way

Jesus also called himself 'the way'. He meant that those who were prepared to follow him were already on the way into the kingdom of God. He said he was like the way or the gate into a sheepfold. The only way into a sheepfold is through the door. The only way into the kingdom of God is through Jesus — by following him and obeying his teaching.
John 14:6 and 10:7–9

Messiah (Christ) and Son of God

It is clear from the Gospels that Jesus was certain that he was the Messiah — the one God had promised to send, and for whom the Jewish people were waiting. But there was a problem. The Jews had a very different idea of what the Messiah would do when he came.

Jesus realized that if he announced himself as the Messiah the people would want to make him fit their ideas. They would try to make him their warrior-leader to free them from the Romans. So Jesus did not announce who he was straight away. Instead, he waited for people to see what he did, to listen to his stories and to understand what he had really come to do.

On just a few occasions the Gospels record a public statement by Jesus saying he was the Messiah and the Son of God. Here are some of them:

★ At his baptism a voice from heaven was heard, saying, 'This is my own dear Son, with whom I am pleased.'

★ When a Samaritan woman said to him, 'I know that the Messiah will come . . . and tell us everything,' Jesus said, 'I am he.'

★ When the religious leaders complained because he had healed someone on the sabbath, Jesus explained, 'My Father is always working, and I too must work.' This made them even more angry, because Jesus had called God his Father.

★ When Jesus asked his disciples who they thought he was, Peter replied, 'You are the Messiah, the Son of the living God.' 'Good for you . . .' replied Jesus. 'For this truth did not come to you from any human being, but it was given to you directly by my Father in heaven.'

★ At Jesus' trial, the High Priest questioned him, 'Are you the Messiah, the Son of the Blessed God?' Jesus replied 'I am . . .'

Son of man

Usually, instead of calling himself the Messiah, Jesus chose to use another name — the Son of man. It was the one he used most often. This was an unusual title which could be taken two ways. It came from a strange figure seen in a dream by Daniel in the Old Testament:

'. . . there before me was one like a son of man, coming with the clouds of heaven . . . He was given authority, glory and sovereign power; all peoples, nations and men of every language worshipped him. His dominion is an everlasting dominion that will not pass away, and his kingdom is one that will never be destroyed.'

By using this name for himself, Jesus was claiming to be the Messiah without using the title. He was also saying he was a human person. (The name can also mean 'human being', as it does in Ezekiel.)

Judge

The quotation from Daniel about the son of man said that this kingdom would last for ever. This was the hardest part of Jesus' teaching for people to understand.

Jesus clearly taught that, one day, the world as we know it will come to an end. 'It will come suddenly,' he said, 'like a thief in the night.'

Because God is just and fair, Jesus taught, a day will come when all the things that are wrong or unfair in life will be put right. Then those who have refused to be part of God's kingdom but have lived for themselves and done wrong things, will be judged and punished.

He also astounded people by promising that one day he would come back to earth himself, but not this time as an ordinary man:

'Then the Son of man will appear, coming in the clouds with great power and glory. He will send the angels out to the four corners of the earth to gather God's chosen people from one end of the world to the other' (Mark 13:26–27).

No wonder people were amazed and shocked by what Jesus said. If a builder and carpenter said something like that today, he would be thought completely mad!

CHECK THE FACTS

You can find the facts about the Messiah in Matthew 3:17; John 4:25; John 5:17; Matthew 16:13–20; Mark 14:61–62.

Jesus' teaching about the end of the world is summed up in Matthew 24 and 25, Mark 13, and Luke 17:20–37 and 21.

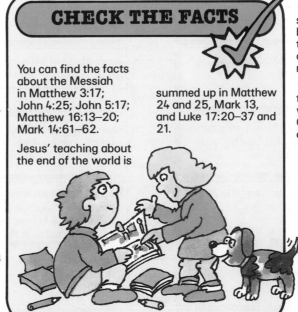

The Jews expected:

★ a special person, sent by God (like the prophets in the Old Testament)

★ someone born in Bethlehem from the family of David

★ a great leader

★ a military general, or at least the leader of a resistance army to defeat the Romans

★ a king for Israel, to bring the country back to God

★ someone to make Israel a great nation and bring peace to the whole world

Jesus was:

★ sent from God, according to the message given to Mary by the angel

★ born in Bethlehem (although not many people knew this)

★ from the family of David, through his mother Mary and Joseph

★ a teacher and healer

★ someone who showed how to love enemies and care for anyone in need

★ someone who suffered and died, to bring the people back to God through a change of heart and mind

★ someone who taught that peace would not come until God's kingdom was complete

SOMEONE SPECIAL

Jesus delighted the crowd with his straightforward common-sense approach to religious teaching. He seemed to bring God near, and to make loving and serving God the most natural and exciting thing in the world.

Of course, this did not make him popular with everyone. The Gospels tell us that the ordinary people loved him. But his popularity made the religious leaders more and more angry. They genuinely thought he was leading the people astray.

Everywhere he went there was gossip and argument about the things he did.

Did you see him touch that leper — with his own hands!

How *could* he. It's not safe.

Fancy walking in the fields on the sabbath and eating some of the ears of wheat!

Just look at the way those kids climb all over him.

That's work! I'm going to report him to the Pharisees.

He tells them stories. Puts ideas into their heads.

Jesus was accepted as a religious leader and given the title rabbi, which means 'teacher'	YET	he was not strictly 'religious' as the rabbis were. His friends were ordinary people and Jesus did not make them obey all the petty rules the Pharisees had developed.
When the rabbis spoke about God they made him sound stern and far away	YET	Jesus spoke about God, clearly and with authority, as if he knew exactly what he was talking about at first hand.
Jesus was a completely good person. No one who knew him well ever accused him of doing anything wrong or unkind	YET	he was easy to be with and had a great sense of fun. Even people the Pharisees called 'sinners' found they could talk to him.
Jesus was a Jew, born and bred, with a mission to his own people	YET	he went out of his way to help Samaritans (despised by the Jews), Romans and Greeks as well as his own countrymen.
Jesus was a man, in a country where women were treated as the property of their husbands	YET	some of his best friends and supporters were women. Jesus talked to women quite naturally and treated them as equals.
Most people respected and feared the religious authorities, especially the Pharisees	YET	Jesus reserved his most biting criticism for some of these people. He called them 'blind guides' trying to lead people, when they understood nothing themselves.
Most people ignored the old, the poor, the disabled and children as being of no importance whatsoever	YET	Jesus cared especially for the poor and the outcasts and spent the largest part of his time with them.

They're saying he's God's Son.

Before he healed that paralyzed man he forgave his sins. Only God can do that!

I tell you, he's not all sweetness and light. I heard he was in a fight last time he went to Jerusalem — in the temple, too. Something to do with the money changers. He attacked them with a whip, would you believe?!

Serves them right, they're always cheating on the exchange rate.

You've got to be joking! Look at the company he keeps. That Matthew's a TAX COLLECTOR!

THE MAN WHO CHANGED LIVES

People who met Jesus were never the same again. Here are just a few examples.

Working fishermen

Peter, Andrew, James and John owned and ran family fishing businesses. Yet they all left their work and went with Jesus until he was put to death.

Later they became leaders of the tiny groups of believers that became the early church. They went on long journeys, teaching, preaching and healing people.

It must have seemed so far away from the shores of Galilee and the small fishing community there.

Crooked taxman

Zacchaeus was a chief tax collector in the town of Jericho. By cheating both his own people and the Romans he had become extremely rich. The people hated him.

He was a short but determined man so, when Jesus was passing by, he climbed a tree to get a better look. When Jesus drew level with the tree he looked up and called Zacchaeus by name. 'Come down, I must stay at your house today.'

After supper, and a long talk with Jesus, Zacchaeus made a dramatic announcement.

'Listen, sir!' he said, 'I will give half my belongings to the poor, and if I have cheated anyone, I will pay him back four times as much.'

That night there was a real celebration at Zacchaeus' house!

Leading Pharisee

Nicodemus was a member of the Sanhedrin, the highest court in the country. He wanted to hear what Jesus had to say. But he was so nervous about his position that he arranged a secret interview after dark.

Jesus respected his need for secrecy and agreed to meet him.

Nicodemus came straight to the point. He said that he believed Jesus had been sent by God because of the way he could heal people.

Jesus told him about God's kingdom. It is like a family, he explained. The only way in is to start again, to be born into it.

Because Nicodemus was a sincere man and a respected religious teacher, Jesus spent a long time talking with him, and from that time on Nicodemus became a secret disciple.

Later, when Jesus was dead, Nicodemus found the courage to come into the open and help with his burial.

A Roman soldier

There was a remarkable Roman officer living in Capernaum in Galilee. He respected the Jewish religion so much that he had paid for a local synagogue to be built.

When one of his trusted servants became ill, he asked the Jewish elders to see if Jesus could help.

He was so confident that Jesus could do it, that he asked him not to come to the house, but simply to give the command.

Jesus was impressed by the Roman. He showed more faith than anyone Jesus had met, even than the Jews. Without going to the house, Jesus made the servant well again. The officer's trust had been rewarded.

CHECK THE FACTS

These four incidents can be found in Matthew 4:18–22; Luke 19:1–10; John 3:1–21; Luke 7:1–10.

If Jesus was here today, would you be for him or against him?

BIG TROUBLE

After three years of going around the country, preaching, teaching and healing people, Jesus knew that his work was coming to an end. He decided to allow his closest disciples to see something that would help them when the inevitable trouble came. He let them see him as he really was. This event — recorded in Matthew, Mark and Luke — is sometimes called the 'transfiguration', which means 'a change in appearance'.

Jesus took Peter, James and John up into the hills where they could be alone. Quite suddenly, Jesus looked different. His face and his clothes seemed to shine with a dazzling light. He was standing talking to two men.

Somehow the amazed disciples knew that the men were Moses, the Law-giver, and Elijah the prophet — two of Israel's greatest leaders from Old Testament days.

As they watched, a shining cloud seemed to come down and cover the figures. A voice came from the cloud: 'This is my own dear Son, with whom I am pleased — listen to him!' They were almost the same words as had been heard at Jesus' baptism.

It was too much for the three disciples. They threw themselves face down on the grass, trembling with fear.

The next moment, someone was gently shaking them by the shoulder. 'Get up,' he said. 'Don't be afraid!' They looked up. It was Jesus, looking just as he normally did. And there was no one else there.

On the way back down the hill, Jesus asked them to keep quiet about what they had seen until after he had been 'raised from death'. At the time, the disciples had no idea what Jesus meant.

Mt Hermon, the high mountain in the north of Israel, is usually believed to be the scene of the transfiguration of Jesus

WHY THE AUTHORITIES WERE AGAINST JESUS

The Jewish authorities, especially the scribes and Pharisees, began by criticizing Jesus for not obeying their religious rules.

★ He broke the rule that banned work on the sabbath. When his disciples walked through the fields on the sabbath, he let them pick off ears of corn and eat them. The authorities said that this was reaping — farming work — and could not be done on the sabbath.

★ He healed people on the sabbath day — sometimes even in the synagogue service! This, too, was thought of as work.

★ He accepted invitations to eat meals with tax collectors and 'sinners', willing to mix with people most rabbis would have avoided.

All these things were serious offences in the eyes of Pharisees. But, in their eyes, Jesus was guilty of even greater crimes.

★ He predicted that the marvellous temple in Jerusalem would be destroyed.

★ He claimed to be the Messiah.

★ He spoke with authority, claiming that his power came from God, his Father! This was regarded as blasphemy — an offence against God.

Some were afraid the Romans would use the excuse of a popular uprising to destroy the Jewish nation. The High Priest summed up the situation: 'It is better to let one man die for the people, instead of having the whole nation destroyed.'

From that moment, they began to make plans to have Jesus killed.

What Jesus said about the Pharisees

Jesus had some friends among the scribes and Pharisees and often accepted invitations to meals in their houses. He knew that many of them were good and sincere men.

But some of them were not, and when Jesus saw them acting wrongly, he did not hesitate to speak out.

He called them 'hypocrites' (a word that comes from Greek theatre and means 'play actor') — people who pretend to be something they are not.

★ 'You are so proud of being religious. You walk about in long robes, wear big 'phylacteries' (boxes containing the Law strapped to the forehead and wrist) and tassled robes.'

★ 'You enjoy religious power. You are bowed to in the street, you take the best places at feasts, sit on the platform at the synagogue and love to be called rabbi.'

★ 'You charge high prices just to say prayers for people even when they cannot afford it.'

★ 'You make so many tiny rules that no one can obey them all. People feel they cannot possibly please God, so they give up.'

★ 'You fiddle about with special taxes on herbs and spices, yet forget the real point of all these laws — true worship of God from the heart.'

★ 'You manage to look so good and religious on the outside, but inside you are as bad as everyone else.'

★ 'You even cheat with your rules. God's Law says that a man should support his parents. But you let him get around it by ''dedicating'' his money to the temple and then keeping it himself!'

Jesus predicts his death

Jesus knew, from very early on, that his work would end in his own death. There was no way around it, because the authorities would not accept his teaching.

But there was more to it than that. Jesus was sure that it was part of God's plan — part of the work he had do.

'From that time on, Jesus began to say plainly to his disciples, ''I must go to Jerusalem and suffer much from the elders, the chief priests, and the teachers of the Law. I will be put to death, but three days later I will be raised to life.'''
Matthew 16:21

At the time they refused to believe Jesus. It seemed impossible that he would let himself be killed. But after it had happened, they remembered his words.

CHECK THE FACTS

At least three times Jesus talked to his disciples about his death. You can find them in Matthew 16:21–23; 17:22–23 and 20:17–19.

Jesus answers questions from the religious authorities; from the film, *Jesus of Nazareth..*

Jesus knew things were coming to a head. The time for teaching was over. It was time to act. He set out for Jerusalem — to celebrate the great Passover Festival and to face whatever lay ahead.

Riding into Jerusalem

Jesus had prepared carefully for entry into the great city. He sent two disciples on ahead with instructions to find a donkey which was ready and waiting for Jesus to ride. As the crowds of people surging towards Jerusalem saw that it was Jesus, they began to chant, 'Praise to David's son!' 'God bless him who comes in the name of the Lord!' 'Praise God!'

They threw their cloaks on the ground in front of the donkey and waved palm leaves in the traditional welcome for an important person.

And some who looked on understood what Jesus was doing. By choosing to ride into Jerusalem on a donkey, he was fulfilling the ancient prediction made by Zechariah in the Old Testament.

'Shout for joy, you people of Jerusalem! Look, your king is coming to you! He comes triumphant and victorious, but humble and riding on a donkey — on a colt, the foal of a donkey . . . Your king will make peace among the nations; he will rule from sea to sea . . .'
Zechariah 9:9, 10

Jesus was claiming quite clearly to be the Messiah that Zechariah had predicted. A humble Messiah who would come in peace.

The plot against Jesus

During the Passover week in Jerusalem, the chief priests and the elders met together. They all agreed that Jesus must die. But it must be done quietly. They needed an 'inside man': someone who knew Jesus well.

Luckily for the authorities, Judas Iscariot was prepared to help. At a secret meeting a price of thirty silver coins was agreed and Judas promised to find a place where Jesus could be arrested secretly.

Jesus rides in triumph into Jerusalem; from the film, *Jesus of Nazareth*.

Instructions and promises

During their last few days together, Jesus spent time with his closest disciples. He had some important things to tell them, to prepare them for the future.

★ He prayed for them, asking God to keep them safe and give them courage.
John 17

★ He promised them that they would never be alone. 'I will ask the Father and he will give you another Helper, who will stay with you for ever. He is the Spirit . . .'
John 14:15–17

★ He also promised that they would be with him, one day, in heaven. 'There are many rooms in my Father's house, and I am going to prepare a place for you . . .'
John 14:2–4

★ He predicted that they would now face all kinds of trouble. 'If the world hates you, just remember that it has hated me first.'
John 15:18

★ They were to live by Jesus' teachings and love each other. 'If you have love for one another, then everyone will know that you are my disciples.'
John 13:35

★ He promised, 'Peace is what I leave with you; it is my own peace that I give you . . . do not be afraid.'
John 14:27

Jesus knew just how weak and human his disciples were. He prepared them for the shocks that were coming, so that afterwards they would know that he understood what they were going through.

★ He predicted that the disciples would run away and leave him when trouble began.
Matthew 26:31–35

★ At the last supper he told them that one of his own disciples would betray him. The others were shocked, but Judas realized that Jesus knew of his plan.
Matthew 26:23–25

★ Peter said, 'I will never leave you, even though all the rest do!' Jesus sadly replied, 'I tell you that before the cock crows tonight, you will say three times that you do not know me, Peter.'
Matthew 26:33–34

A detailed account of Jesus' last instructions can be found in John chapters 13–17

THE LAST SUPPER

Jesus planned his last Passover meal with his friends very carefully.

Because of the danger, they had to meet in secret. Jesus booked an upstairs room in Jerusalem and Peter and John were sent on ahead to prepare the meal.

The traditional Passover meal

This meal is still eaten by all orthodox Jewish families, to remember the time when Moses led them out from slavery in Egypt. It begins with a prayer and the blessing of the first cup of wine.

Then each person takes herbs and dips them in salt water. The father of the family takes one of the three flat cakes of bread made without yeast, breaks it in half and puts some aside.

Next the story of the Passover is remembered and a Psalm sung. The second cup of wine is then passed around.

Usually at this point the family wash their hands, ready for the meal.

To begin the meal, grace is said and the bread distributed. Bitter herbs dipped in a big bowl of sauce are then given around. A meal of roast lamb follows. This special Passover lamb reminds the Jews of the lamb killed by each family in Egypt on the night of the first Passover.

At the end of the meal, the family sings some hymns together and the fourth cup of wine is passed around.

The Passover story

The people of Israel had become slaves in Egypt when God called Moses to challenge the king (Pharaoh) to let them leave. He refused. God gave him many opportunities to let the people go peacefully, but it took ten terrible disasters before he agreed. The last was the death of the firstborn son in every Egyptian family.

To protect themselves, the Israelites were told to kill a lamb and mark the doorways of each house with its blood. When the Angel of Death visited the Egyptians, he 'passed over' each house marked with the blood of the lamb. That is how the festival came to be called the Passover.

A special meal

Jesus made some important changes to the traditional Passover meal that night:

★ Jesus went further than the washing of hands. He tucked a towel around his waist and washed all his disciples' feet. (This was usually done by a slave as the guests arrived at a gathering.)

When they asked why he did this, Jesus told them that he was setting them an example of humble service. This was how they should treat each other in future.

★ Half-way through the meal, Jesus took the bread that had been put aside, broke it and handed some to each man. 'Take and eat it,' he said. 'This is my body.'

★ Jesus took a cup of wine, handed it to each disciple and said, 'Drink it, all of you; this is my blood which seals God's covenant (or agreement), my blood poured out for many for the forgiveness of sins.'

Jesus used the bread and the wine in this way, to show that he was the new Passover lamb, ready to give up his own life to save people from death. He asked his followers to continue this special meal, to remind them of what he had done for them. Today it is called the Lord's Supper, Eucharist, Holy Communion or the Mass.

Accounts of the Last Supper can be found in Matthew 26:20–29; Mark 14:17–25; Luke 22:15–38; 1 Corinthians 11:23–25.

Christians today share the bread and wine of 'the Lord's Supper' in memory of Jesus' sacrifice for them.

COUNTDOWN

The events of the last weeks of Jesus' life on earth can be found in all four Gospels: Matthew 21–28; Mark 11–16; Luke 19:28–24:53 and John 12–21.

Sunday

Jesus rides into Jerusalem on a donkey

He sheds tears as he predicts that Jerusalem will be destroyed

He returns to Bethany for the night

Monday

Jesus enters the temple and throws out traders

Tuesday

Jesus teaches in the temple courtyard and argues with the Pharisees and Sadducees

He goes to the Mount of Olives, overlooking Jerusalem. He talks about the end of the world

Wednesday

The religious authorities plot Jesus' death. Judas joins them

Jesus speaks to the crowds for the last time

At supper in Bethany, Mary pours perfume on Jesus' feet as a special gift

Thursday

Preparations are made for the Passover in Jerusalem

Jesus' last supper with his friends — the Passover meal

Judas leaves to plan Jesus' arrest

Jesus and the eleven cross the Kidron Valley to Gethsemane. Jesus prays for strength to face his death

ARREST, TRIAL AND SENTENCE

After the Passover supper, Jesus took his disciples to a place called Gethsemane. Jesus wanted to pray quietly before the coming troubles. But his friends were so miserable at what was happening that they could not concentrate. They huddled together, waiting for Jesus, and fell asleep.

Jesus prayed on his own, pleading with God to find another way to deal with people's wrongdoing.

Worse than torture and death was the thought of having to be parted from his Father God, while he took the punishment for all the wrongdoings of the world. The pain of that would be much worse.

Sweating with agony at the thought, Jesus finished his prayer, 'If my death *is* the only way, then I will do what you want.'

The trap

As Jesus went to wake his disciples he could hear a crowd approaching. A figure stepped out of the shadows.

'Jesus!' cried Judas, giving him his usual bear-hug and kiss on the cheek. It was a signal. Seconds later a large group of soldiers grabbed Jesus.

'Why all this secrecy?' Jesus asked the priests and elders, who now took charge. 'Why swords and clubs, as though I were an outlaw? I've been in the temple every day and you didn't try to arrest me!'

The next few minutes were chaos. The disciples fled into the darkness. Only Peter followed, well hidden, as the prisoner was hustled back into Jerusalem, to the High Priest's own house, to face a series of hurried unofficial trials through the night, for fear that those who supported Jesus might start a riot.

Trial 1

Jesus was first questioned about his teaching by Annas, the High Priest's father-in-law.

Jesus replied, 'I have always been open, teaching in the synagogues and in the temple. Why don't you ask my followers what I taught?'

A soldier hit Jesus across the face for speaking so boldly to the High Priest.

What happened to the disciples?

After the arrest in Gethsemane, **Judas** deeply regretted what he had done. Matthew records that he gave the money back to the elders and committed suicide.
Matthew 27:3–9

John says **Peter** and another disciple managed to get into the courtyard of the High Priest's house, where Jesus was being questioned. As they waited, three different people asked Peter if he was one of Jesus' followers. Peter was so frightened that he denied it. Then the cock crowed and Peter remembered that Jesus had predicted he would let him down. He was so ashamed that he broke down in tears.
John 18:15–18, 25–27;
Mark 14:66–72

Trial 2

Annas then sent Jesus to Caiaphas the High Priest, and the Sanhedrin Council.

Two witnesses said that they had heard Jesus say he would destroy the temple and build it again in three days! But they could not make their stories agree. When questioned about this, Jesus would not reply.

Caiaphas decided on the direct approach. 'In the name of the living God,' he said, 'I now put you on oath: tell us if you are the Messiah, the Son of God.'

'I am,' Jesus replied, 'and you will all see the Son of Man seated on the right of the Almighty and coming on the clouds of heaven!'

A ripple of excitement went around the group of elders. The prisoner had committed 'blasphemy' (a crime against God) in front of the court!

Anyone who blasphemed should be stoned to death, but the Romans would not allow the Jews to execute anyone. If they wanted Jesus dead, he must be tried by the Romans.

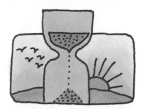

Torches flare in the darkness: Jesus is betrayed; from the film, *Jesus of Nazareth*.

As the trial ended, the temple guards were allowed to humiliate Jesus, beating him and spitting on him.

Trial 3

Jesus was brought to the Roman Governor (Procurator) of Judea, Pontius Pilate.

This time the Jews accused Jesus of treason against Rome — by telling people not to pay taxes to Caesar and claiming to be King of the Jews.

Pilate asked Jesus, 'Are you the King of the Jews?'

Jesus replied, 'My kingdom does not belong to this world; if my kingdom belonged to this world, my followers would fight to keep me from being handed over to the Jewish authorities. No, my kingdom does not belong here!'

'Are you a king, then?' asked Pilate. 'You say that I am a king,' said Jesus. 'I was born and came into the world for this one purpose, to speak about the truth. Whoever belongs to the truth listens to me.'

Pilate was not convinced that Jesus deserved to die. He heard Jesus was a Galilean, so he tried to get out of sentencing him by sending him to Herod Antipas, ruler of Galilee, who was in Jerusalem for the Passover.

Trial 4

Herod was keen to meet Jesus. He had heard amazing things about the preacher and hoped to see him do a miracle. Jesus remained completely silent, refusing to answer a single question.

Disappointed, Herod sent him back to Pilate — after another beating.

Trial 5

Back in the Roman court, Pilate tried again to free Jesus. It was usual for one political prisoner to be released at the Passover Festival. Pilate offered Jesus, but the crowd shouted for Barabbas, a well-known rebel leader.

Finally, as the crowd appeared to be near to rioting, Pilate agreed to the death sentence for Jesus. But he ordered a slave to bring a bowl of water into the courtroom. In front of them all, he washed his hands, to show that he did not approve of the sentence.

Condemned man

Once the sentence was given, Jesus was flogged (tied to a pillar and beaten with leather whips which had pieces of metal at the end). Then he was handed over to the army.

The soldiers had heard that Jesus was supposed to be king of the Jews. They dressed him up in a purple robe, made a crown from some thorny branches, and bowed mockingly before him.

COUNTDOWN

Thursday night

Judas leads guards to Gethsemane. Jesus is arrested; disciples scatter

Jesus tried by the High Priest and Sanhedrin Council

Peter follows Jesus to the house; denies being a disciple

Early Friday

Sanhedrin take Jesus to the Roman Governor

Judas commits suicide

Trial by Pilate

Jesus sent to Herod Antipas for trial

Sent back to Pilate, who tries to release him. The crowd shout for Barabbas instead

Pilate gives the death sentence but washes his hands of the whole affair

Jesus is flogged, mocked and prepared for crucifixion

Jesus was crucified outside Jerusalem, on Skull Hill (Golgotha). The words 'Jesus of Nazareth, King of the Jews,' were written in Hebrew, Latin and Greek, and fixed to the cross for all to read.

A small group of disciples, together with Jesus' mother Mary, were standing a little distance away. They heard Jesus pray for his enemies, 'Forgive them, Father! They don't know what they are doing.' He also asked John to take care of his mother.

Two criminals were crucified at the same time. One joined with the crowd, who were laughing at Jesus, saying, 'Aren't you the Messiah? Save yourself and us!' The other told him off and said, 'Remember me, Jesus, when you come as king!' Jesus said to him, 'I promise you that today you will be in Paradise with me.'

Just before he died, Jesus cried out, 'My God, my God, why have you abandoned me?' — words from Psalm 22:1. Then he said, 'It is finished!' He prayed, 'Father into your hands I commit my spirit!' and died.

Dead and buried

When the soldiers came to break the victims' legs (to speed up their death) they were astonished to find Jesus already dead. They speared his side, to make sure. John says that he saw blood and water come from the wound.

The bodies had to be buried before sundown, when the Passover sabbath began. Joseph of Arimathea, a respected member of the Jewish Council, asked for permission to bury Jesus. He planned to use the new family grave he owned.

Fellow council member Nicodemus and a small group of women came too, bringing burial spices and sheets to wind around the body.

The burial was a hurried affair. When it was finished they rolled the great stone door into place, sealing the tomb.

Later, the Jewish Council made things doubly sure by sealing the stone and posting a guard of soldiers outside.

WHY DID JESUS

At first, Jesus' disciples thought his death on the cross was a terrible mistake. But, later on, they remembered he had spoken about his death as something that *had* to happen. At their last supper together, he had said his blood would be 'poured out for many for the forgiveness of sins'. What did he mean by this?

The bad news

Jesus taught — as the Old Testament teaches — that God is a God of love, but he is also 'good' and 'holy'. This means that he can have nothing to do with evil or wrongdoing of any kind. So the fact that we keep doing wrong things has made friendship with God impossible.

Because God is holy, he can't just overlook wrongdoing. Things must be put right — just as, when someone takes another person's property, or even another person's life, the law decrees that they must be punished.

But because God is also loving he has done something about it himself. In one of his most famous sayings, Jesus put it like this:

'God loved the world so much, that he gave his only Son, so that everyone who believes in him may not die but have eternal life.'

The good news

This explains why, at the worst moment on the cross, Jesus said, 'My God, my God, why have you abandoned me?' He was knowing what it is like no longer to be friends with God — to be separated from him. Jesus was taking the punishment for everyone.

As a result, everyone who depends on Jesus rather than themselves,

CRUCIFIXION

Crucifixion was a terrible death. The Romans crucified slaves, foreigners and criminals, but not Roman citizens.

To the Jews, it was the ultimate disgrace — the criminal died under God's curse.

The condemned person had to carry his own cross-beam. The upright post was already in the ground.

The victim was stripped and his wrists tied or sometimes nailed to the cross-beam before it was hoisted up and fixed to the upright. The feet were tied with leather strips or were nailed. A block of wood half way up the cross supported the weight of the body.

A notice with the name of the criminal, his home town and his crime was fixed to the cross.

It could take as long as three painful days to die in this way.

The crowd gathers outside the Governor's palace to hear Pilate's sentence on Jesus; from the film, *Jesus of Nazareth*.

COUNTDOWN

Friday

Jesus carries the heavy wooden cross–beam until a passer-by is forced to help

Roman soldiers crucify Jesus; his mother and disciples look on

There is an unnatural darkness from noon till three, when Jesus dies

The earth quakes and the curtain at the entrance to the 'holy of holies' in the temple rips from top to bottom. Strange events reported in Jerusalem

Soldier pierces Jesus' side with spear to make certain he is dead

Joseph of Arimathea and Nicodemus hastily bury the body in Joseph's family tomb

Roman guard posted at the tomb

HAVE TO DIE?

can be forgiven. They enter God's kingdom. They become friends with him for ever.

This is why the day on which Jesus died is remembered each year as 'Good Friday'. His

death was not a mistake but a once-for-all victory in the fight against evil and death. And three days later, he was alive again to prove it!

Jesus is crucified between two criminals; from the film, *Jesus of Nazareth*.

CHECK THE FACTS

The events of Jesus' death and burial are listed by all four Gospel writers: Matthew 27:27–61; Mark 15:16–47; Luke 23:26–56; John 19:1–42.

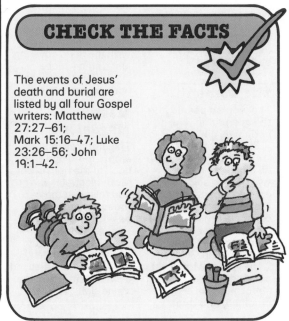

THREE DAYS LATER

At break of dawn, on the first day of the week, some of the women who had been followers of Jesus arrived at the tomb. They expected it to be just as they had left it on Friday night, when they had helped Joseph and Nicodemus bury Jesus' body.

They had brought more burial spices, and were discussing how they could get the great stone rolled back from the entrance, when they stopped in amazement. The stone appeared to have been moved. The grave was open!

What happened in the next few hours was so unexpected and frightening for the disciples, that it is difficult to piece together the exact order of events. But this is what the Gospels say about the different individuals involved.

The joy of Mary Magdalene that Jesus is alive again is caught in this picture from the film, *Jesus of Nazareth*.

The guards

Matthew says that an earthquake rocked the hillside early that morning. As if this wasn't enough to frighten the guards on duty at the tomb, an angel appeared like a bolt of lightning and rolled back the great entrance stone. The guards were paralyzed with fear.

When they had gathered their wits, they rushed back to the city with the bad news.

However, instead of being punished, they were given a large sum of money and told to spread the story that Jesus' disciples had stolen the body!

The women

The women peered into the open tomb. The body was gone!

Shocked, they looked around and saw an angel (or was it two?), who said, 'Why are you looking among the dead for one who is alive? He is not here; he has been raised. Remember what he said to you in Galilee: ''The Son of Man must be handed over to sinful men, be crucified, and three days later rise to life.'''

Leaving the tomb, the women rushed back to tell the other disciples what had happened.

Peter and John

The disciples were still huddled together behind locked doors when the women arrived with their amazing news.

At once Peter and John set out for the tomb. As they peered into the darkness inside the cave, they saw the linen cloths that had been bound around the body lying with the head covering just a small space away. But there was nothing inside them!

Mary Magdalene

The disciples left the empty tomb and went back to the house. But Mary Magdalene, who had followed them to the tomb, stayed beside the entrance, crying quietly.

As she glanced up she saw two angels, like young men dressed in white, sitting on the stone slab. 'Why are you crying?' they asked.

'They have taken my Lord away, and I do not know where they have put him!' sobbed Mary.

Then a voice behind her asked who she was looking for. Thinking it was the gardener, she said, 'If you took him away, sir, tell me where you have put him, and I will go and get him.'

'Mary!' said Jesus.

Instantly Mary knew it was Jesus — not dead, but fully alive. She clung to him, crying with joy and relief.

'Don't hold on to me,' said Jesus gently, 'because I have not yet gone back to the Father. But go to my brothers and tell them that I am returning to him who is my Father and their Father, my God and their God.'

CHECK THE FACTS

Matthew 28:1–15; Mark 16; John 20:1–18.

DID IT REALLY HAPPEN?

Many people find it hard to believe that Jesus actually came back to life in the way the Gospels describe.

Over the years there have been several other explanations of what happened.

1

'Jesus was not dead — he merely became unconscious on the cross and revived later in the cool tomb'

BUT:

★ Jesus was crucified by Roman soldiers who knew their job. They were satisfied that he was dead.

★ If he did revive in the tomb, he would have been a very sick man.

He would have had to roll back the heavy entrance stone.

★ He would have had to lie to the disciples, or else get them to agree to lie about what had happened.

★ He would have had to live in secret until he really did die.

2

'Someone stole the body'

BUT:

★ The robbers would have had to get past the guard and the sealed stone.

★ No one had a motive for stealing the body. The Romans wanted a quiet life, not more

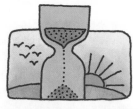

Back to life again!

On the night Jesus died, the disciples were the frightened, disappointed followers of a man who had turned out to be a failure. Three days later, they were sure he was the Son of God, alive and well because death could not keep him down! His coming back to life made all the difference to Jesus' followers.

★ It changed their whole attitude to Jesus.

★ It gave them good news to tell everyone. They were eye-witnesses to the most amazing event and they wanted to tell people.

★ Jesus had predicted his death and that he would come back. If he was right about this, everything else he said should be true too.

★ It convinced them that Jesus was the Messiah, God's Son, because they were certain that power over death could come only from God.

★ It made possible the new agreement between God and his people. God had accepted Jesus' 'sacrifice'. The accounts of how his followers spread this good news, became known as the new 'testament' or 'agreement'.

Rich people often had family tombs carved out of solid rock. A large stone could be rolled across the entrance to close it. This picture is from the film, *Jesus of Nazareth*.

COUNTDOWN

Saturday

The sabbath rest day

Sunday

Stone is rolled back from the entrance of the tomb. An angel appears. The guards are shaken rigid with fear

Women arrive at dawn, with sweet-smelling spices for the body. They speak to two angels

Women tell Peter and John, who run to the tomb, enter it and see wrapped grave clothes, but no body inside

Mary Magdalene returns to the grave and meets Jesus

Guards report to the chief priests. They are bribed to say the body was stolen

Two disciples walking to Emmaus see Jesus. They hurry back to Jerusalem

Jesus appears to the disciples (all except Thomas) and eats with them

---

religious excitement. The Pharisees also wanted the body safe in the tomb, which is why they had it guarded. If they had taken the body, they could have produced it as soon as the disciples started saying that Jesus was alive. It would have silenced them once and for all.

The disciples were not expecting Jesus to come back. If they had taken the body, they would have had to live with the secret all their lives. They could never have gone out to tell people Jesus had risen from death, with his dead body hidden somewhere — and been prepared to die for it.

Ordinary thieves would not want a crucified man with no possessions. And they would never have gone to the trouble of unwrapping the corpse. (We are told that the grave clothes and head cover were left in the tomb.)

3

'The women went to the wrong tomb'

BUT:

★ Joseph of Arimathea would have been able to put the matter right. It was his tomb.

★ Even if *all* the disciples got the wrong tomb, the Jewish authorities could have pointed out the right one, complete with body!

DOES IT MATTER?

The disciples were thrilled to see Jesus alive on the first Easter day, not only because he was their friend, but because it proved to them his claim to be God's Son. He had said he would come back to life — and he had!

So the first thing they wanted to tell people was the startling news that Jesus had come back from death. Peter, speaking to the crowds in Jerusalem, put it like this:

'In accordance with his own plan God had already decided that Jesus would be handed over to you; and you killed him by letting sinful men crucify him. But God raised him from death, setting him free from its power, because it was impossible that death should hold him prisoner.' Peter told them he had seen Jesus alive with his own eyes: 'God has raised this very Jesus from death, and we are all witnesses to this fact.'

Paul, one of the earliest Christian teachers, put it even more clearly: 'If Christ has not been raised from death, then we have nothing to preach and you have nothing to believe.'

It really mattered to those first Christians that Jesus had broken the power of death and come back to life. His death and resurrection was at the heart of the 'good news' they preached everywhere they went.

You will find the words of Peter and Paul in Acts 2 and 1 Corinthians 15.

Jesus appears to his disciples in the Upper Room. Can he be real? From the film, *Jesus of Nazareth*.

After the shattering events of that Passover weekend, Jesus' disciples were in a state of confusion and shock. Both Luke and John mention that on the first day of the week — the day that is now called Easter Sunday — they met together in the upstairs room in Jerusalem, behind locked doors.

The news that some of the women, and then Peter and John, had found the grave empty, followed almost immediately by Mary Magdalene saying that she had seen Jesus alive, threw them into even more confusion. The Gospels describe several more events which show the disciples' growing astonishment and wonder, as they began to be convinced that Jesus really had risen from death.

That night, two of Jesus' friends (one was called Cleopas), were walking sadly back to Emmaus — about 11 km/7 miles from Jerusalem.

A man joined them, and started asking them questions about what had been happening. It was late and they invited him to stay. It was not until he said grace at their meal, that they recognized Jesus!

They were so excited, they rushed all the way back to Jerusalem and began to tell the others. Suddenly they fell silent. Jesus himself was standing in the middle of the room!

'Peace be with you!' he said.

The disciples were terrified, but Jesus showed them his hands and side, where they could see the marks made by the nails and spear. He also ate some fish, to convince them that he was not a ghost.

John records that they were '. . . filled with joy at seeing the Lord.'

Thomas

One man was not with the others in the upstairs room that night. When Thomas heard that Jesus had appeared, he found the whole thing hard to believe. 'Unless I see the scars of the nails in his hands and put my finger on those scars and my hand in his side, I will not believe,' he said.

A week later, the disciples were all together again. The doors were securely locked, but Jesus was suddenly there among them. He turned to Thomas.

'Put your finger here,' he said, 'and look at my hands; then stretch out your hand and put it in my side. Stop your doubting, and believe!'

'My Lord and my God!' stammered Thomas.

'Do you believe because you see me?' asked Jesus. 'How happy are those who believe without seeing me!'

Peter

Soon after the Passover, the disciples went home to Galilee. Peter, James and John and some of the others decided to go fishing. They caught nothing all night. As the sun came up, a man standing on the shore called out to them, 'Throw your net out on the right side of the boat, and you will catch some.' They did so, and could not haul it back in because of the catch. 'It's Jesus!' said John.

Jesus had built a fire and cooked their breakfast, just as he used to do. It was great for the disciples to spend time with Jesus in the countryside they knew so well. And one disciple particularly needed to talk.

Peter felt terrible about the way he had let Jesus down in Jerusalem. Jesus knew this, and on the shores of the lake he spent time helping Peter to accept that he had been forgiven and was being given special work to do.

The Gospels say that for forty days, Jesus appeared to his disciples from time to

A small fire burned on the shore, as the disciples returned from a night's fishing. And there was Jesus, inviting them to breakfast!

time. But he began to explain that he must now leave them to go back to his Father in heaven.

He repeated the promise, made to them at their last supper together, that the Holy Spirit (God's own Spirit, living with them and in them) would be there to help them. They were to wait in Jerusalem for him to come.

Then Jesus took the disciples with him to the hillside at Bethany, where they had so often stayed. There he said goodbye. The last words of Luke's Gospel say, '. . . he raised his hands and blessed them. As he was blessing them, he departed from them and was taken up into heaven.'

Just ten days later, the disciples were together in a house in Jerusalem. It was the Feast of Pentecost (the Jewish festival of Firstfruits which came at the beginning of the wheat harvest). Jerusalem was crowded with visitors from all over the Roman Empire.

Suddenly, there was a noise like a strong wind. It seemed to blow right through the house. And what looked like flames of fire touched each person.

The effect on the disciples was astonishing. Each person ran outside, eager to tell everyone what he had seen and heard about Jesus. And they were able to speak in different languages, so that the multi-racial crowds understood them!

People were pressing forward, trying to see what was going on. 'They're drunk!' said someone, seeing the excited faces of the disciples.

Finally Peter stood up and spoke to the crowds. He told them that the Holy Spirit, long promised in the scriptures, had finally come. And that Jesus, whom they had allowed the Romans to kill, had come back to life because he was God's Messiah.

He spoke with such power urging everyone to ask for God's forgiveness and receive the new life he offered, that Luke records some 3,000 people were added to the group of Jesus' followers that day. The Christian church had been born.

Jesus' last messages to his friends

'I have been given all authority in heaven and on earth. Go, then, to all peoples everywhere and make them my disciples: baptize them in the name of the Father, the Son, and the Holy Spirit, and teach them to obey everything I have commanded you. And I will be with you always, to the end of the age.'
Matthew 28:18–20

'This is what is written: the Messiah must suffer and must rise from death three days later, and in his name the message about repentance and the forgiveness of sins must be preached to all nations, beginning in Jerusalem. You are witnesses of these things. And I myself will send upon you what my Father has promised. But you must wait in the city until the power from above comes down upon you.'
Luke 24:46–49

CHECK THE FACTS

You will find the account of what happened at Pentecost in Acts chapter 2.

We have looked at the remarkable life of Jesus of Nazareth, his country and birth, his friends and the way he lived. We have seen the kind of things he did, the way he helped people and the things he taught them.

We have read about how and why he died. And we have heard the disciples' accounts of how he came back to life.

Obviously someone who behaves like this is not an ordinary person. So it is worth asking who Jesus really was.

A lot of people say that Jesus was a very good person and leave it at that. But if we look carefully at what Jesus said about himself, we have to face the fact that he claimed to be much more than that.

'Who do you say I am?'
Matthew 16:15

Everyone can choose whether or not to believe and trust Jesus and enter God's kingdom.

Jesus said he was the Messiah, God's Son, sent by God to make forgiveness and a new life possible for all who believe in him.

Either

1 OR **2** OR **3**

he was lying or pretending

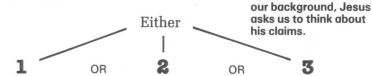

the Jewish authorities were right to have him executed

Jesus was a liar

he honestly believed he was God's Son, but he was wrong

he would be diagnosed today as mentally ill and given treatment

he was a sad case because he was crucified for his crazy ideas

Jesus was a lunatic

it was true

he lived a life that backed up his claims

he died of his own free will, to bring people back into friendship with God

he came back to life and returned to heaven, as he said he would

Jesus is God's Son

These children, all from one school, share twenty-four different languages! No matter who we are, or what our background, Jesus asks us to think about his claims.

What about today?

Jesus' followers obeyed his instructions to tell everyone the good news about him. Today over 1400 million people in countries all around the world believe and follow Jesus. And this makes all the difference to the way they live. There is a meaning and purpose to life. Jesus inspires many people today to make a difference to the world in which they live.

In the 1960s Baptist Minister **Martin Luther King Jr** led a protest movement against the way black people were treated in the United States. Jesus taught that all people are equal in God's sight. The laws against black people were unjust, and Martin Luther King set out to change them. He believed that a follower of Christ should not use violence to achieve his goals, so he determined to fight by non-violent means.

Eventually the battle was won and black people achieved equal rights with whites, but it cost Martin Luther King his life. In 1968 he was assassinated.

The same kind of battle is going on today in South Africa. There **Archbishop Desmond Tutu** of Johannesburg, and Christian thinker, **Dr Alan Boesak**, with many others, have boldly spoken out against the unfair treatment of non-white peoples.

Other church leaders such as **Dom Helder Camara** of Recife, Brazil, **Archbishop Oscar Romero** of El

Salvador, **Cardinal Sin** of Manila in the Philippines and **Archbishop Luwum** of Uganda have followed Jesus' example and stood up for the poor and oppressed in their countries.

Football international **Glen Hoddle** says:
'I realized that it was all true — what the Bible says about Jesus . . . God *is* changing me.'

Mother Teresa of Calcutta cares for the poor and the dying in her homes in India.

She believes that Jesus' love for each individual should be shown in caring for the very poorest people in society.

These are just a few examples of Christians who make the headlines in the cause of justice and a better world today. There are many thousands more that we never hear about.

As well as in public life and politics, there are people in the world of the arts, entertainment and sport who admire Jesus' example and teaching. And many claim to know that he is alive today.

Bono Vox, lead singer with the band U2, says:
'I think that people know my belief that Jesus Christ is very real in the twentieth century. That's in my music and my music is my life.'

Soul singer **Deniece Williams** says:
'When you remember that Jesus is the star of your life and not you, it kind of helps you to put things in a better perspective — you are a servant.'

Singer **Philip Bailey** describes meeting Jesus for himself:
'That night I knew beyond a shadow of a doubt that Jesus Christ was real. I felt like my sins had been washed away.'

But Jesus' influence extends further than just the well-known and the high-powered. Today there are people from every walk of life who follow him and try to put his teachings into practice.

QUIZ

Use this quiz to test your memory, at home or in school. The answers are all in this book.

1. Where was Jesus born?

2. What was King Herod's reaction when he heard about the baby Jesus?

3. Where was Nazareth?

4. At roughly what age did Jesus begin his work?

5. Who was John the Baptist?

6. What does 'Gospel' mean?

7. Why did Jesus refuse to turn stones into bread?

8. What was a zealot?

9. Name three disciples and their jobs.

10. When did Jesus find the time to pray?

11. What kinds of illness are we told that Jesus could cure?

12. What did the Jews mean by the 'Messiah'?

13. What was the Sanhedrin?

14. Who sold Jesus to the authorities?

15. How long was Jesus in the tomb?

16. Why is the Friday before Easter called 'Good Friday?'

17. Who was the first person to see Jesus alive after he had been killed?

18. What convinced the disciples that Jesus was not a ghost?

19. Name one Christian who has made a difference to the modern world.

Answers on the next page.

Index

Answers to the Quiz

1 Bethlehem in Judea.

2 He ordered the death of all baby boys in the Bethlehem area.

3 In the hills of northern Palestine, in the region called Galilee.

4 About 30 years of age.

5 Jesus' cousin and a religious preacher and teacher.

6 'Good news.'

7 Because he did not want people to follow him just because of his miracles.

8 A political group dedicated to ridding the country of the Romans.

9 Peter, Andrew, James and John were all fishermen; Matthew was a tax collector.

10 Very early in the morning.

11 All kinds of illness.

12 A prophet, a military leader and a king, who would set them free and make them great.

13 The Jewish high council, allowed to rule under Rome.

14 Judas Iscariot, one of Jesus' disciples.

15 From Friday night, until early Sunday morning.

16 Because it is the day on which Jesus died for everyone in the world.

17 Mary Magdalene.

18 He let his disciples touch him and ate a piece of fish to prove he was not a ghost.

19 You will find some on **20**.